Katie Jerram's

MODERN HORSE MANAGEMENT

Katie Jerram and Carolyn Henderson

J.A. ALLEN · LONDON

First published in 2015 by
J. A. Allen
Clerkenwell House
Clerkenwell Green
London ECIR OHT

J. A. Allen is an imprint of Robert Hale Limited
www.allenbooks.co.uk

ISBN 978-1-908809-27-8

British Library Cataloguing in Publication Data
A catalogue record for this book is available from the British Library

Edited by Martin Diggle
Design and typesetting by Paul Saunders
Photographs © John Henderson,
except for the photograph on page 48 © Mirrors for Training
Line drawings on page 103 © Maggie Raynor

Printed by Craft Print International Ltd, Singapore

With thanks to my parents, who taught me so much
and continue to help in so many ways.

Contents

CHAPTER 1

Blueprint for Modern Management

THE REALITIES OF MANAGEMENT

At first glance, horse management might seem to be a rather cold and impersonal term. But at its heart is the reality that everyone who is responsible for a horse's day-to-day care has a huge responsibility.

No matter how much we care for our horses in an emotional way or how much we strive to keep their lifestyles as close to nature as possible, we manage every minute of their lives. We choose where they live, when and what they eat, how much socialisation they enjoy, the type of exercise and training they undergo and the athletic pursuits they follow. Caring for horses can and should be part of our management philosophy, but we must never forget that if a horse is unhappy about an aspect of his lifestyle, he can't change it. It may be tempting, especially on a busy yard, to organise everything for human convenience, but that may not always be the most effective and therefore the most efficient regime.

No matter how fond of a horse you are, he is nearly always a working animal rather than a pet. It doesn't matter whether he is primarily a competition horse or a family friend: he has a job to do. To do that job, whether it be hacking or horse trials, to his full ability, he needs to be healthy, happy, sound and confident in his work.

Management is at the heart of a horse's well-being. Modern owners and those who work in the equestrian industries have knowledge and research at their fingertips that was unknown even fifty years ago and we

◀ ▲ Whatever a horse's job, he must be healthy, happy, sound and confident in his work.

may feel we know better than our predecessors how to protect a horse's well-being. For instance, at one time, a horse who was a weaver, wind-sucker or crib-biter would be condemned as having a vice and 'managed' by sometimes inhumane methods. Now, we know that 'stable vices' are stereotypical behaviour patterns that, in general terms, are a horse's reaction to being confined.

We may still confine horses by keeping them at least part of the time in stables and it may be that, in practical terms, this is sometimes essential. However, we now accept, or should do, that fitting a collar which induces discomfort or pain when a horse arches his neck to crib-bite, or even putting him through surgery to sever nerves which make this possible – which at one time was considered a feasible 'solution' – cannot be justified. Instead, we look at ways of organising the horse's routine and environment to make any periods during which he may have to be stabled as acceptable as possible.

Against that, we also have to guard against letting well-meaning ideals over-rule common sense. It's all very well saying that horses are born to live outdoors 24/7 and, at base level, this is true. But when a horse is in hard work and has to be clipped and his field is so wet and churned up that he is fetlock-deep in mud, a compromise may be the best option on both sides, and a mixed regime of turnout in a suitable area combined with stabling will often be the best for everyone involved, two- and four-legged. 'Natural' is not always synonymous with good: it might be natural for horses to be outdoors in all weathers, but it's

also natural for them to go hungry when conditions are bad, and to be eaten by predators.

Just as importantly, we must work out the principles of good management but, at the same time, look at every horse as an individual. That skill marks the difference between someone who is a good horse manager, whether on a private or commercial basis, and someone who is conscientious but not quite doing the best for and therefore getting the most out of a horse.

That is where this book comes in. Whether you are a private owner wanting to do the best for your horse and get the most from him, a student looking forward to a career in the horse world, or someone who already runs a yard, I hope you'll find in this book ways to improve your horse management skills. They may require you to analyse why you follow practices you've carried out for years and, perhaps, change some of the ways you operate. They may also reinforce some principles that have been the bedrock of horse management for many years, albeit by including new techniques.

The advice in these pages comes from years of private and commercial horse management and has been proven to work for horses and ponies of all shapes, sizes and roles. The methods have been applied to show horses, racehorses, eventers, youngsters starting out their careers and even children's ponies. The result is a long and continuing roll-call of happy, healthy and successful horses. If you didn't care for horses, you wouldn't be reading this book; by continually striving to improve your management skills – as we all should – you will be doing the very best you can.

SAFETY FIRST

Horse-related accidents are more common than you might think. The only statistics available relate to riding accidents but, as anyone involved with horses knows, you don't have to be in the saddle to be potentially at risk.

Whether you are a one-horse owner or manage a large yard, it's essential to do all you can to ensure that everyone stays as safe as possible. The consequences of accidents don't just affect the individual: employers have a duty of care and, in both private and commercial set-ups, litigation is common. Individuals who have been injured by horses have brought civil cases against their owners even when most reasonable people would assume that an owner could not be held responsible and, whatever the outcome, litigation leads to stress.

Today's teachers and employers have to talk in terms of making risk assessments, being properly equipped and following best practice. In simple terms, this means having horse sense and common sense.

The most successful riders, handlers and trainers know how to think like a horse. They understand how horses react and don't anthropomorphise. For instance, a horse who spooks when a bird flies out of the hedge isn't being naughty, he's reacting to an unexpected stimulus in the way nature intends. Horses are prey animals, so when they are frightened, they run away from the source of fear rather than confronting it.

I always find it amusing when riders come for lessons and complain that their horse is 'being naughty and won't canter on the right leg/rein-back'. Horses don't wake up and decide to wind up their riders or handlers – if they don't give the response you wanted, either you haven't asked correctly or the horse is physically incapable of obeying the instruction.

A horse who behaves aggressively is a different matter and must be managed with extreme care. He needs experienced, professional-standard handling by someone who is calm, can react quickly and quietly when necessary and will not become angry. In my experience, many horses who seem to be aggressive are actually frightened of you and the key is to get them on your side whilst ensuring that you stay safe.

Sometimes, an aggressive/nervous horse will react badly if you make eye contact with him. In this case, I walk quietly towards him but keep myself turned slightly to the side so I am not confronting him. I approach slowly and calmly and, when I make contact, put my hand on his shoulder. I don't just walk in, look at him and try to put my hand on his head – to him, that's confrontation.

I've never had a horse who didn't come round, but you must always be aware of how this type of animal reacts. Monitor his routine and identify what he does and doesn't like. Remember, too, that perfume – even a perfumed deodorant – can set off a reaction, especially if it has a musky smell. Don't wear perfume or aftershave and make sure anyone else handling him follows the same rule. If you're an employer, never let inexperienced staff – or anyone you can't trust to be constantly aware and confident – to handle such a horse.

You may also find that, occasionally, a horse will take a dislike to another on the yard beyond the normal behaviour of establishing a pecking order. In this case, don't stable them next to each other and don't turn them out together.

Throughout this book, I'll give examples of safe practice. For starters, here is a list of basic, sensible strategies:

▪ Wear safe clothing, particularly headgear, when handling as well as riding horses. I'm riding and working with horses all day, so put on my hat first thing and only take it off if I have a lunch break. If your current hat seems hot and/or uncomfortable, shop around for a new one. The latest lightweight safety hats and helmets are very comfortable and I forget I've got mine on.

Safe, comfortable footwear is another must. No one expects you to wear smart leather boots when mucking out – and if you do, they won't last, because the ammonia in horse urine and droppings will ruin them – but yard boots should be supportive, have soles which give sufficient grip and be easy to put on and take off. Some designs are marketed as being safe for working and riding, but don't ride in boots which have tread soles, even if you use safety stirrups, as they might not give a quick enough release.

▪ You may be in control of your horse, but you can't always be in control of what's going on around you – so pay attention to what you're doing, not to the text message that's just come through as you're leading your horse out to the field.

▲ The latest safety hats and helmets are lightweight and comfortable.

▪ Be confident and consistent. Horses are herd animals and a horse will – or should – look to you as his leader. If you are calm and confident, you stand a good chance of him being the same.

Be consistent in what you ask for and what you expect and it will pay dividends in your horse's behaviour and attitude, under saddle as well as in hand. The top in-hand show producers insist that their horses always walk out correctly when being led and never let them slop along. At the same time, be fair. Don't expect a horse to stand and be trimmed up at a time when he's used to being fed.

Don't take routine tasks and well-mannered horses for granted. If you drape a lead rope over a horse's neck rather than tie him up with a proper quick-release knot, don't be surprised if he shoots across the yard when a passing car backfires.

■ Horses thrive on routine when they are at home and soon get used to how a yard is run. It gives them security, so if possible, establish what happens when and try to stick to that. Some people maintain that you shouldn't provide this security blanket because it can't be followed on competition days but, in my experience, horses accept that show days are different from home days. I've found that routine is particularly important when dealing with Thoroughbreds who have come out of racing, as they are used to regimented lifestyles.

■ A horse can hurt you without meaning to. He can stand on your foot or strike out with a front or back leg when something startles or irritates him – and if you're in the wrong place at the wrong time, hard luck.

The answer is to always try to be in the right place and to make sure that a horse knows where you are. Speak to him as you approach him and make

▶ Horses from a racing background are very much used to a routine.

your approach from an angle which allows him to see you. Horses have a blind spot directly behind them. They also have monocular vision and see things out of one eye at a time rather than through both eyes. That is why a horse may walk past something, spook and regain his equilibrium, but then spook again when he walks past it in the other direction. He isn't being stupid; it's because of the way his eyesight passes information to his brain.

Never kneel next to a horse, because you're vulnerable to being knocked over or trodden on. Bend down, so you have a better chance of being able to jump out of the way if necessary.

Also, make sure your arm is in front of the horse's cannon bone when you pick up a hind leg. If you position your arm behind his leg and he kicks out, you are in line for a broken arm.

■ Horses react strongly to scent; the Flehmen's reaction, where the top lip is curled upwards, amuses us because it gives the impression that the horse is laughing. However, there is a sac at the top of the nasal passages called the vomeronasal or Jacobson's organ which horses use to get more information about a particular smell. By curling the top lip, he partially closes his nostrils, which helps to block off other scents. Don't underestimate the effect that the sense of smell can have. As mentioned earlier, never wear perfumed products when working around stallions, as some become excited by it. Nor should you put a rug worn by one horse on another without washing it, as some will be disturbed by the 'wrong' smell.

■ Handle a horse from both sides, not just from the nearside. We're taught to tack up, mount and lead from the left, but this encourages a horse to always bend to the left. It also means that if you need to lead him on the road, where the British Horse Society advises walking on the left-hand side with the leader between the horse and the traffic, he is accustomed to being controlled from the right.

■ Sometimes, you will need to think for others as well as for yourself. If you are on a yard where there are children and/or dogs, be aware of where they are and what they are doing. If the dogs and/or children are yours, train them! At the same time, you have to accept that an excited child or dog may, for example, forget not to run behind a horse. My dogs are on the yard with me and I look on that as being part of my horses' education, but I'm also careful to keep them out of the way when necessary.

■ Don't be afraid to ask for help. There are many occasions when it's safer, easier and quicker for two people to carry out a task than for one to risk trying it alone. Inexperienced employees should not be asked to handle horses known to be difficult, though it may benefit them to gain the experience of helping, under the supervision of the yard manager or another more experienced member of staff.

■ If you're a private owner and know that your horse is difficult in a particular respect – the obvious examples are when being clipped or loaded – don't try to manage alone. Ask a professional with a good reputation to help as, once a horse's fear or objections have been overcome in a kind but sensible manner, you will hopefully be able to take over. Make sure you ask someone with recognised skills and a well-earned reputation rather than someone who claims to be a 'horse whisperer' or similar.

KEY POINTS

- We manage every minute of our horses' lives and must be aware of that responsibility.

- Good management is at the heart of keeping a horse happy, healthy and sound.

- It's good to establish principles, but ideals should not overrule common sense.

- Horses have common instincts and needs, but are also individuals.

- Whatever you are doing, safety must come first.

CHAPTER 2

A Stable Environment

A horse's environment has a huge effect on his health and well-being, both physical and mental. Physical considerations mean that he must be provided with a safe environment that minimises the risk of injury and disease and gives him protection from adverse conditions all year round. Psychologically, he must feel safe and relaxed.

A lot is talked and written about keeping horses as nature intended. Certainly, we must remember that we are dealing with an animal who relies on his instincts, even though horses have been domesticated for 6,000 years. Unfortunately, so much has been said and written about the necessity of keeping horses the 'natural' way that it's easy to lose sight of three important points.

The first is that the modern horse is a working animal, whether he is a top-class athlete or kept purely so that his owner can have the pleasure of looking after him and hacking or driving him without competing. Every horse, whatever his job is or was – because retired animals should be treated as well as working ones – should have the best possible level of care.

The second point is that, when trying to keep horses in a natural way, it's very easy to romanticise the existence of the wild horse. Nature isn't all about green fields and an idyllic existence; it's about survival. Keeping a horse out 24/7 in all weathers in an established herd, which is often held up as the ideal management system, can and does work for some. However, it demands a large area of suitably managed land and most horse owners simply do not have that available.

▲ Two or three compatible horses will live amicably together.

Nor is it possible for many yards to keep an established herd. If you keep two or three horses at home you may build up an established group, but commercial and competition yards will find that impossible. They usually have a changing equine population, either because clients move away or send horses for limited periods to be schooled or competed, or because horses are sold. Selling horses is a fact of life for most professional competitors, even if they don't like doing it. Not every horse makes the grade and producing horses for sale is, for most professionals, a necessary way of helping to fund their careers.

The third point is that horses, like people, are individuals. Some may seem to dislike being stabled, though with thought, the right facilities and adequate turnout this can usually be overcome. I've never had a horse whom I couldn't stable part of the time and be confident that he was relaxed and happy, though I accept that not everyone has access to different options within the same yard, as I do. There are many horses who look on their stable as a home and are always ready to come in when the weather is bad or when they are irritated by insects, despite every care being taken to repel flies and mosquitoes. Again, turning a stable into a home takes thought and the ability to assess a horse's personality and reactions, as explained later in this chapter.

In deciding how we can give a horse the nearest-to-perfect environment, I believe we should accept that, in most cases, a regime which mixes time out in the field with time in the stable is the best of both worlds, not a compromise. There are strong views on how best to keep horses and those who see the issue in black and white and are passionate to the point of becoming zealots are not helping horses or owners.

STABLE YARD LAYOUT

There are as many types of stable yard as there are types of housing, from long-established yards with their own sense of history to state-of-the-art set-ups more akin to an equine hospital. Each has advantages and disadvantages, but I feel I have the perfect set-up for my job, which ranges from backing young horses to producing top-level competition animals. In its time, my yard has housed point-to-pointers, event horses, show animals, children's ponies, broodmares and foals.

It's a set-up that has grown over the years, as the original yard needed to expand. That has become its greatest strength as, rather than one large,

▲ Few yards could match this one in Newmarket for luxury – but horses can be just as happy in less palatial surroundings.

impersonal yard I have smaller, satellite ones branching off my original one. This enables me to find a slot that suits a particular horse. For instance, those who prefer a quiet environment can lodge on a small, quiet square of boxes, whilst those who enjoy constant mental stimulation and like to see what's going on are happiest in stables where they have a good view of horses being worked in the nearby school. As there's usually something going on, from lungeing to gridwork, they never get bored.

This might seem an old-fashioned arrangement compared with a purpose-built competition yard or an American barn set-up, but it works. American barns may save time and therefore money because everything is under one roof, but there are disadvantages as well as advantages, as discussed later in this chapter.

Where there are horses, there is muck. Our muckheap is on a concrete base and is sited so it can be removed easily and regularly and does not cause a nuisance either to us or our neighbours. It is also kept in good shape.

My feed room is light, airy and has a wash-down tiled floor. This makes it functional and easy to keep clean, which is important for the sake of hygiene and to discourage vermin. Similarly, my tack room is out of sight of casual visitors, one of several necessary security measures. My tack does not get damp or mouldy, partly because the tack room environment minimises the risk of damp and partly because all tack is checked and cleaned regularly. We have a hay store that allows us to keep hay in dry, well-ventilated conditions and use bedding wrapped in waterproof packaging, which can be stored outside.

▶ My round pen is ideal for loose-schooling and introductory work.

▶ My horse-walker is used as an addition to exercise, not a substitute for it.

Our arena is a short walk from the stables and visible from some fields and stables. We also have a horse-walker used as an addition to exercise, not as a substitute, and a round pen, used for loose-schooling and for introductory work with horses being backed.

BETTER BY DESIGN

If you are building a yard from scratch, you have a wonderful chance to design a layout for your exact needs. Don't just rely on theory: visit lots of yards – old and new, specialising in different disciplines – and ask owners what they couldn't do without and what, in hindsight, they wish they had included. If possible, talk to the staff who work there, too, because they may identify different pros and cons.

Building projects can soon rack up horrific costs and most people, including those working on a commercial scale, have budgetary constraints. However, one of the commonest mistakes is not identifying priorities and trying to do everything at once on an inadequate scale rather than leaving some things until later. It's all too easy to make false economies, even on a small scale: many owners of two horses will wish they had built three stables rather than two, as the cost of the third would have been much smaller had it been built at the same time rather than leaving it until they needed extra space.

Work out what you need to operate efficiently and safely from the start: that's your A list. Your B list should comprise additional facilities and equipment you aim to add later and which your initial plan should take account of. As part of this, ask whether a particular facility is a luxury, or something which would make your or your staff's work easier, quicker and therefore cheaper. Heat lamps and/or wash boxes are not cheap, but in some circumstances could earn their keep quickly.

We all want to have high standards, but creating the right impression can be practical as well as pleasing. Hopefully, clients will not be impressed by hanging baskets rather than happy horses, but a yard with a pleasing outlook and safe facilities reinforces the message that the person running it is knowledgeable and conscientious.

Those who are taking over or want to make the most of existing facilities usually have less freedom than those who can design from scratch. However, they should still identify good and bad points and get expert advice on making adaptations. Don't assume that older yards are inferior to modern ones: they often have solidly built, well-ventilated stables that provide a healthier environment than some modern constructions and are more likely to stand up to wear and tear.

GETTING PERMISSION

Planning constraints must be considered and can be a nightmare. Never assume that you can build or adapt without getting planning permission; it may not always be necessary, but if you go ahead, the worst scenario is that you could find yourself facing a fine and being forced to demolish a new building or restore one to its original specifications. (*NB Points made on planning-related topics in this chapter are based on UK legislation, but other countries will have their own planning laws and readers resident outside the UK should be sure to check the pertinent legislation.*)

Sadly, it is increasingly difficult to obtain planning permission for permanent brick stabling and permanently sited field shelters. This is largely a result of unscrupulous tactics by people who applied for permission to build stables when they had no intention of horses being anywhere near the buildings. Before planning officials got wise to the trick, stables would be built and change of use applications followed swiftly, the intention being to turn them into living accommodation.

Many authorities now refuse most applications for brick stabling and will only allow wooden stables. One benefit of adapting an existing set-up may be that you find more success in getting permission to turn existing brick buildings that have had an agricultural use, such as dairies or machinery stores, into stabling even though UK legislation does not class horses as agricultural animals. If you live in a green belt area, you may find it easier to obtain permission for change of use and modification of existing buildings than for building new ones.

The only permitted use of most rural land in the UK is for agricultural purposes, which, as just mentioned, does not include keeping horses. Whilst the grazing of horses on agricultural land does not constitute a material change from a former agricultural use, anything beyond grazing would require planning permission. Some councils have even ruled that the temporarily siting of showjumps on fields requires planning permission – and installing an arena would generally require it even if it is for private rather than commercial use.

There are exceptions, but it is always safest to use a specialist planning consultant, especially when making applications. Stable manufacturers and arena specialists will not usually make applications on clients' behalf, but are used to the requirements and should be able to help by supplying drawings and photographs to show what the installation will look like. Getting professional help will allow you to make the right impression, show that you will not be causing problems for neighbours and other users of access roads and dispel any misconceptions. Most councils give free pre-planning advice but, in some circumstances, you may need to consult a solicitor who specialises in planning law.

The horse's non-agricultural status and the fact that councils in some areas of the UK – particularly the densely populated south-east – are worried about 'horsiculture' (a term now widely used to mean commercial use of the countryside for keeping or exercising horses), makes life as difficult for owners making genuine equestrian applications as for those trying to sneak granny flats under the planning radar.

It also means that owners in some parts of the country are not allowed to have field shelters sited permanently on grazing land. This should be easier to overcome, as there are many designs of mobile shelter on skids, which can be moved at required intervals. However, you should still check planning regulations, as mobile shelters fall into a grey area. If you are lucky enough to have fields bounded by thick, natural hedging, these may supply sufficient shelter, but modern farming practices means such hedging is becoming rarer and additional forms of shelter are usually needed.

STABLE CHOICE

In many situations, one of the biggest decisions you need to make is whether to have conventional looseboxes or indoor stabling. For simplicity, I'm using the term indoor stabling as interchangeable with American barn; technically, the latter is a purpose-built construction and indoor stabling is often a conversion of an existing large building by adding walls and partitions, sometimes made to measure.

From the human point of view, indoor stabling has much to offer. It enables you to stay dry and relatively comfortable when carrying out routine care such as mucking out. It also wins on a time and motion study basis, as horses and equipment are under one roof.

However, it may not be so successful from the equine point of view. It isn't always easy to ensure good ventilation – though specialist manufacturers and architects can help – and in theory, it is more difficult to prevent the spread of disease, as germs and viruses spread rapidly when horses share the same

◄ American barns make a great working environment for people, but in theory, it is more difficult to prevent the spread of disease.

airspace. In practice, this is a problem with any set-up unless hygiene and management protocols are top class.

For instance, although I make it a rule that I must be on site whenever a new horse arrives at my yard, whether on a permanent or short-term basis, things occasionally go wrong. As this book was in preparation, the owner of a horse I had agreed to take in for backing sent him a day early without warning. I returned home to find the transporter had insisted on leaving the horse and my staff had put the animal into an isolation box. They got top marks for doing so, but I wasn't pleased by a message that had been left via the transporter to tell me that the horse 'had a few spots, but they weren't ringworm'. The horse did, in fact, have ringworm and I told the owner that he must be collected the following day. As I explain in Chapter 10, ringworm is not a dangerous condition, but it is inconvenient and, on a professional yard, potentially an expensive nuisance. It spreads like the proverbial wildfire and I will not take in a horse if I have the slightest suspicion that he has ringworm anywhere which may bring him into contact with others. The 'slightest suspicion' factor is not, incidentally, a matter of being over-cautious – you don't always get visual warning of an outbreak, as the incubation period is usually between four and fourteen days (though it can be longer) and a horse may arrive looking perfectly healthy and break out afterwards. As it was, we instituted preventive hygiene measures immediately (also explained in Chapter 10) and there were no cases in our yard.

STABLE BASICS

The basic requirements of any form of stabling are that it should provide sufficient room, good ventilation and an environment in which the horse is safe and comfortable.

Stable dimensions are calculated on floor space and the *minimum* dimensions quoted are often:

Pony up to 148 cm (14.2 hh) – 3.05 m (10 ft) square

Horse up to 162 cm (16 hh) – 3.65 m (12 ft) square

Horse over 162 cm (16 hh) – 4.26 m (14 ft) square

Broodmares about to foal/with foals at foot ideally need a stable at least 50 per cent larger than the mare alone would require. Ask your vet's advice.

Internal headroom should be a minimum of 3.65m (12ft) to give reasonable ventilation and big horses should ideally have more. Door openings should be at least 1.22m (4ft) wide, whatever the size of the occupant, to minimise the risk of an animal banging his hip as he goes in or out. Doors must be of suitable height for the animal to be able to see over without having to raise his head and neck at an unnatural angle, so a Shetland pony needs a door scaled or suitably adapted to Shetland dimensions. All stable doors should open outwards.

Whenever a horse is stabled, he is in an environment that carries dust and spores. This is inevitable, no matter how well-designed the stabling and how meticulous your management. Scientists now know that a huge percentage of horses have some degree of recurrent airway obstruction (RAO), a term that has largely replaced the former one of chronic obstructive pulmonary disease (COPD). This adds weight to the premise that horses should spend as much time turned out as possible but, as we have already discussed, you have to look at the big picture. Accommodation is an important part of that, but not the only consideration. Rather than getting stressed over the fact that you have to stable your horse part of the time, work out how you can make his environment as healthy as possible.

In terms of stable design, this means providing ventilation measures that offer frequent air exchanges, but in a way that minimises the risk of draughts. If a horse cannot escape draughts he will be uncomfortable, which may result in muscle stiffness and tiredness. Think how you feel when you've had a poor night's sleep: why should a horse be any different?

Whether you are dealing with a new-build project or existing buildings, a window in the back of the stable as well as one in the front is an excellent and relatively inexpensive way of providing extra ventilation, as long as you manage

◀ An extra window gives the stabled horse a more interesting outlook.

the options this provides to minimise the risk of unwanted through-draughts. As already mentioned, this also gives the horse a more interesting view on life.

Roof pitch and the number and siting of air outlets must be taken into consideration. The best way of finding the right arrangements for your situation is to consult an expert with technical and equestrian expertise. Stable manufacturers are much more clued up about ventilation than they used to be, but ask what measures they use and why when deciding which company to employ, and beware anyone who dismisses the issue as unimportant.

Walls should be lined with kickboards, preferably full height, which add insulation and protect the external structure from at least some damage. Even unshod hooves go through most kickboards remarkably easily, so consider using wall mats if necessary – but ask why a horse is using what, to him, is a defence mechanism. Is he kicking because he is worried or annoyed by his neighbour? Look at the cause, not just the effect.

The best way of dividing stables depends on individual set-ups. If you have a static horse population and congenial horses, using bars at the top half of a dividing wall may help you keep occupants content. If you have a changing population – which applies to many competition yards – you may not want horses to be able to sniff at their neighbours because of health issues and the risk of incompatibility between individuals.

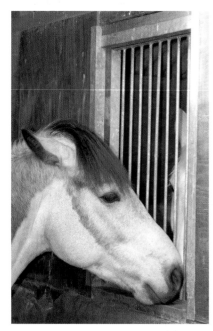

▼ Bars at the top half of a dividing wall may work with congenial neighbours, but not if one horse tries to bully another.

Drainage is important, as ammonia from urine and droppings affects a horse's respiratory system. Again, you need to look at your whole management picture, as bedding materials, efficiency of mucking out and ventilation are all parts of the same jigsaw: the best drainage system won't work if drains are allowed to become blocked. It is often said that efficient drainage relies on there being a slight fall (slope) on the floor which allows liquid to drain away to an appropriately sited outlet, but this is not always present in older buildings – or, sometimes, in newer ones where stable bases have been built without specialist knowledge.

If you are planning a new set-up or have problems with an existing one, get specialist advice and consider whether or not you are using bedding which best suits your needs. Rubber matting is widely used and I recommend it, always with supplementary bedding unless your vet specifies otherwise. Some horses are reluctant to stale (urinate) on matting alone and it's impossible to keep rugs clean if horses are bedded that way, but most mats will need to be removed regularly and the floor underneath cleaned and disinfected.

FIELD SHELTERS

Horses need protection from wind and rain in cold weather and from flies in the summer. If trees and hedging do not give sufficient natural shelter, you need to supply a purpose-built one. Conventional designs are basically open-fronted stables, but the opening must be large enough to allow more than one horse at a time to have safe access and exit, or arguments and injuries may result. You may also find that whilst some horses use this type of shelter, others are reluctant to do so and will stand outside, using a shelter wall as a windbreak. This may be a natural preference or it may be that the horse is being intimidated by field companions.

A less common design comprises windbreaks made from solid 2m (6ft 6in) sections laid out like wheel spokes. Horses use these happily but need appropriate rugs to protect against the cold and wet or against insects.

◄ Field shelter openings must be large enough to allow more than one horse at a time to have safe access and exit.

► Some animals prefer this type of windbreak.

As with stables, check whether you need planning permission. If getting permission for a permanent shelter is a problem, look at mobile ones. These are built on skids and can be towed by a tractor or ordinary four-wheel drive vehicle. Because they can and should be moved at irregular intervals, they have so far been exempt from planning permission.

FIXTURES, FITTINGS AND INDIVIDUALS

Mangers, water containers and tying-up rings are standard fixtures and fittings and are often taken for granted. Think about how you position them so you site a horse's feeding and watering stations in a way that suits him. It's the equivalent of choosing to sit in a quiet corner of a restaurant or in a place where you can see everything that's going on – only your horse can't choose and has to rely on you.

If a horse doesn't relax whilst he eats his feed and hay, he may be stressed because he doesn't feel safe – perhaps because he doesn't have privacy on a busy yard, or from his neighbour – or because he needs to know what is going on and keeps moving between his feed and the door.

I use corner mangers for feed and water and position these and haynets at the front or back of the stable according to the horse's behaviour. Some like to eat in privacy whilst others prefer to eat and watch. A few prefer to dunk and watch, taking a mouthful of hay, then dunking it in their water to soak it to their satisfaction.

Insecure horses may be worried if their neighbours' mangers are sited close by, even if there are solid walls between the two. Putting the mangers of adjacent stables in opposite corners is good standard practice.

The most natural way to offer feed and hay is at ground level, as it mimics grazing and protects the natural grinding pattern of the teeth, but it is also wasteful. I prefer to use haynets and mangers, positioned safely but not so high that the horse has to stretch his head and neck awkwardly. I have never had problems using this approach as I compensate for possible disadvantages through my overall management strategies; for example, regular dental checks and maintenance.

Large yards often use automatic watering systems to save time, but I prefer the hands-on approach. If automatic systems are used, they should be the type that includes individual gauges so you can assess how much a horse is drinking. It's important to spot signs of dehydration early and, with automatic waterers without measurement gauges, you can't assess intake. If using automatic systems, it's very important that supply pipes are protected against freezing, and that they are shielded from potential damage by horses.

Should you use grilles to deter stereotypical behaviour: in particular, weaving? I use V-shaped grilles as standard, not particularly to deter a horse from weaving but to discourage him from trying to jump over a stable door. Horses don't seem to mind them, but a determined weaver will simply stand back and weave behind the door.

▶ V-shape grilles discourage horses from trying to jump over a stable door.

It used to be thought that horses copied others on the yard who demonstrated weaving, crib-biting or wind-sucking behaviour, but scientists say this is not so. If a horse already has the predisposition to show the behaviour, he may copy it, but if he hasn't, he won't. We also recognise that labelling these behaviour patterns as stable vices is unhelpful and unfair, as a horse is instinctively acting to release natural stress-releasing hormones (endorphins).

Crib-biting is the most unpopular form of stereotypical behaviour, because it puts wear and tear on both structures and horses. Traditional strategies include fitting collars designed to make the behaviour uncomfortable, or painting unpalatable substances on the surfaces the horse preferred to grip. There have even been anti-cribbing devices that 'work' by giving the horse a mild electric shock when he latches on to a surface, which I hope no one would consider using.

Again, I've found that by providing the horse with an environment in which he can relax, stereotypical behaviour can be reduced and in some cases, even eliminated. Horses rarely weave when turned out and some will only crib-bite when confined. If a horse always cribs on the same surface, such as a door or window ledge, fastening a piece of rubber cut from an old tyre will reduce damage to his teeth and the surface.

Consider trying a stable mirror which, for safety reasons, should always be made for the purpose from specially toughened material. There is a lot of anecdotal evidence that mirrors act as a calming influence and in some cases, reduce or eliminate stereotypical behaviour. It is thought that horses see their reflections as companions and as such, they must be introduced with care; some horses may see the 'intruder' as a threat, at least to start with.

KEY POINTS

- If you are building from scratch, visit other yards in all disciplines and talk to owners about what they like and what they would like to change. Learn from others' experiences and mistakes.

- Work out priorities to identify essential needs, facilities you can install later and the difference between realistic wishes and dreams. Where possible, aim for quality over quantity.

- Always find out whether you need planning permission. This applies to new-build and change of use projects.

- Look at stables from horses' point of view as well as considering the comfort and convenience of those who look after them.

- Pay attention to the choice and siting of fixtures and fittings so you can alter where you put a horse's feed and water.

CHAPTER 3

Field Choice and Management

As most owners keep their horses at livery rather than owning or renting grazing land, this chapter may seem to be of academic interest to some readers. However, even if you are never called on to manage and maintain your horse's grazing, you must be able to recognise whether it is suitable or safe.

GENERAL CONSIDERATIONS

Standard advice is that you need a minimum of 0.4 hectares (1 acre) per horse to keep land in good condition all year round, bearing in mind that horses are herd animals and should not be kept alone. In practical terms, that area can be reduced in the case of small ponies, but once you go below this practical area per occupant you increase the risk of accidents and squabbles if one horse feels threatened by another and can't get out of the aggressor's way.

There may be times when you need to restrict grazing, but it's important to do this in a way that keeps a horse happy. As the most common reason for this is to prevent a horse becoming obese and to avoid the associated health risks, strategies are suggested in Chapter 5, which deals with feeding.

Grazing land has two roles, both of which require it to be well maintained. As a turnout area, it enhances your horse's well-being, allowing him to move around, mix with compatible friends, relax and even play. As

▶ A field should provide suitable grazing and the chance for a horse to relax and even play.

a food source, it is the natural choice – grass is what horses are designed to eat, even though there may be times when you need to restrict intake.

Pasture quality depends on the type of land, the varieties of grass sown, stocking density and maintenance. All types of land have pros and cons and the best policy is to get expert advice from someone who understands both land management and the needs of horses. Just as importantly, ensure that your expert knows how to work your type of soil. General guidelines are useful, but don't always work across the board.

There are many good agricultural contractors who can, if necessary, help with maintenance work, but if you are seeding or re-seeding, you need someone with equine knowledge. Advice must be based on practical experience of managing the relevant type of land, as general principles aren't always adequate. For instance, if you have light land which cuts up easily, you may need to sow grass seed at a higher density than is routinely recommended, to ensure a strong root mat and resilient sward.

Most grassland in the UK is sown for cattle and the food value needed to produce milk or beef is very different from that needed by horses. Many owners have to keep their horses on cattle pasture, but to minimise the risk of obesity and laminitis, this usually demands strategies such as strip-grazing – restricting a horse to a small area, which also restricts his movement – or using a grazing muzzle to limit grass intake. There is more information on this in Chapter 5.

If you are sowing grass to create a new field for horses, or repairing damaged areas, choose grass species that are compatible with horses' nutritional needs, the type of land and even climate conditions. Whilst flooding has become a common hazard in some parts, spring and summer droughts are a handicap in others. Land that has been flooded usually takes a long time to recover, but in persistently dry areas, talk to a grass seed specialist about drought-resistant species.

Many seed merchants have grass mixes designed specifically for equines. A typical mix could comprise half timothy, meadow fescue and creeping red fescue and half perennial ryegrasses to give a dense, hard-wearing sward. If you wish, you can add a herb mix, but you can't guarantee that your horse will eat the result!

▲ Grass species should be compatible with horses' particular needs.

SAFETY FACTORS

Horses often seem as if they are accidents waiting to happen, so fields must provide a safe environment as well as food and relaxation. One of the best ways to keep horses safe is to ensure that everyone involved in their care remains observant. That way, hazards such as broken fencing, rabbit holes, poisonous plants and debris can be dealt with immediately.

Good fencing is essential and if you have thick hedging that provides shelter as well as a barrier, count your blessings. Alternative choices include classic post and rail, permanent and temporary electric fencing and stock fencing with wire mesh designed to be safe for horses. The latter is designed so that a horse should not be able to get his foot caught, as can happen with sheep or pig fencing.

Gates must be in good condition and well balanced, so they are easy to open and close. You don't want to have to struggle with a gate and with a horse who is anxious to go out, as this endangers both of you. In a perfect world, gates are ideally not sited at the lowest part of the field, which is likely to be wettest, but this is not always possible. If soggy gateways cause a problem, consider putting tarmac planings or special matting down.

Poisonous plants can kill and, every year, horses die from poisoning caused by ragwort, acorns and other hazards. Ragwort is a biennial plant, so destroying it takes at least a two-year programme – sometimes longer, as seeds can remain dormant in the soil for up to twenty years. During the first stage of

▲ Post and rail fencing with offset electric wire.

◄ Wire fencing with a top rail, designed especially to be safe for horses.

growth, it forms rosettes that lie flat to the ground and are easily missed; the bright yellow flowers appear in the second stage. The best way to remove it is to dig it up using a special ragwort fork and then to burn it away from the field. Always wear gloves, as blood tests have shown that the toxins it contains may enter the human bloodstream if it is pulled or handled without protection. On large areas, removing ragwort by hand may be impractical and you will have to rely on chemical methods. Products and application methods vary so, again, get advice on the appropriate strategy for your circumstances.

Yew is deadly and there have been cases of horses collapsing and dying after eating a single mouthful. It isn't usually chosen to border grazing, but is common in churchyards – so if you have a field next to a church, be aware. You may need to add internal fencing inside the normal field boundary to make sure horses keep their distance.

If you have oak trees in or bordering your grazing, then ideally, either take horses out when acorns fall – which is usually around October–December – or temporarily fence off a large area around the trees and collect the acorns before grazing it again. Sycamore seeds are also potentially fatal and their ingestion has been linked to atypical myopathy, a muscle disease. These seeds are so light

Plants that are poisonous
to horses:

1. Ragwort in flower
2. Ragwort in the rosette stage
3. Buttercups
4. Bracken
5. Acorns
6. Sycamore seeds
7. Nightshade
8. Yew.

35

that they are easily wind-borne and can travel long distances from the parent tree, so the only safe strategy is to take horses out of fields that put them at risk during danger periods.

Other harmful plants include foxgloves and members of the nightshade family, which can be lethal when ingested in sufficient quantities. Don't assume that plentiful grazing makes poisonous plants less of a danger, as it has been found that some horses seem to seek out ones with a bitter flavour.

Buttercups are by no means as big a danger as the plants detailed above, but heavy growths should be sprayed off. Eating large quantities of buttercups has been implicated in some cases of colic and may also cause blisters around the mouth area.

PASTURE MANAGEMENT

The most essential pasture management task is to remove droppings as often as possible, mainly because this breaks the parasite circle and so reduces a horse's worm burden. This can be done by hand over small areas, but large fields call for specialist paddock-cleaning machines. Research shows that ideally, droppings should be picked up at least every two days, but this may not be practical.

Traditionally, harrowing is carried out to break up droppings and so speed up the breakdown process. Unfortunately, this also spreads worm eggs over a larger area. If it is the only option, harrow only during periods of very hot weather, so that the UVA rays in sunlight kill the eggs. If your soil is light, harrowing brings the extra risk of pulling out so much plant material that you are left with bare patches where weeds will flourish. However, when land will stand up to harrowing, it encourages grass to tiller (grow more leaves per stem), which increases its ground cover and discourages weeds.

Pasture management could more accurately be described as damage limitation and means fighting a constant battle against a horse's natural grazing habits. To get the most out of your field, you need horses to graze it as evenly as possible, but they prefer short grass to long. They also naturally use some parts as toilet areas, which they prefer not to graze. This results in roughs and lawns.

The best ways to encourage horses to graze more evenly are to top long grass to a height of around 7.5cm (3in) and/or to graze cattle or sheep on the land. Grazing with sheep can be especially beneficial, as they act like four-legged rollers. Their feet firm up the ground without doing damage and they will clear ivy and other plants that you don't want on horse pasture, but which do not harm sheep. The other advantage of grazing with cattle or sheep is that they will help clear the worm burden, as worms do not cross species.

Rolling with machinery helps press down and so firm up land that has become cut up, but you should take the drainage properties of your soil type into account. Heavy soils, particularly clay, may be compacted by rolling to an extent that drainage is compromised.

Weeds soon spring up in bare patches, so the more you can do to avoid land being poached, the better. This usually requires a balancing act between managing stocking density, re-seeding bare patches after winter and, if possible, resting fields or parts of them rather than grazing continuously.

Fertilising should be done with caution to minimise the risk of obesity and laminitis. If it's essential, use a fertiliser formulated to encourage steady rather than speedy growth. Herbicides may be essential at times, but some products can only be applied by suitably qualified farmers or contractors. In some cases, horses must be kept off fields for a specified time after a herbicide has been used.

It's impossible to prevent land being damaged by hooves, especially when horses are shod. Realistically, you can only do your best to protect both horses' needs and your grazing. Horses need freedom to move and young horses, in particular, need the opportunity to play. It's no coincidence that sales of calming supplements rise during the winter months when some yards have limited turnout!

If turnout time in the field has to be curtailed, can you use an alternative area such as an arena or a round pen, even if only for short periods, to allow horses to stretch their legs and have a roll? Hay will keep them occupied and nutritionists suggest that if you want to mimic natural grazing habits, you should tie several haynets in different places to provide different feeding stations. However, you also need to ensure that haynets can be tied at a safe height, to minimise the risk of a horse pawing at and getting a foot caught in a net. It's safer to feed hay from the ground, but if leavings are trampled into the surface, this can affect your arena's drainage – so every time you use it as a turnout area, collect any hay that remains.

Some horses will be happy turned out in a school in compatible pairs, whilst others will start play-fighting or more serious squabbling and must be turned out alone. However your horses behave, using a school this way will add to wear and tear on the surface and result in some areas getting heavier use than others. This means it's important to level the surface regularly, though this may already be a daily task on a busy yard.

GRAZING GROUPS

Opinions vary on how groups of horses should be organised when they are turned out. Many people prefer to put mares in one field and geldings in another, on the grounds that some geldings still show an interest when a mare is in season or will try to keep others away from her. They believe that keeping the genders separate reduces disputes and injuries. My system is to turn horses out in pairs rather than in groups and to base pair selection on what I hope will be compatible temperaments rather than gender.

A lot is said about pair bonds and natural herd environments. When horses are kept together for some time they do forge herd hierarchies and even friend-ships, but many commercial yards, including livery yards, have a changing horse population. When horses are kept in groups, the safest way to turn out a new arrival is to introduce him by turning him out in a small field or fenced-off area next to the group he will eventually join, with either a quiet pony or the gelding who is lowest in the pecking order in the main group. Hopefully, once the established residents have got used to the 'new boy' he can be introduced to the main group without too much hassle. There will still be some jostling for position, but it's a lot safer than opening the gate, letting in a new horse and hoping for the best.

Some commercial yards graze each horse in a very small, separate paddock where he can see other horses and, if fencing allows, enjoy mutual grooming. This is better than no turnout, but not as beneficial mentally for a horse as an environment that allows him space to have a good canter if he feels like it. However, some horse owners will blame yard owners for any misfortunes that occur even when every care is taken, so there may be circumstances when this system is a compromise between the ideal and a yard owner's need to minimise the risk of aggravation or even litigation.

Commercial yard owners may also use this system purely because clients send horses to them for short periods for schooling and they don't have time to check compatibility and can't risk turning them out as part of a larger group. There may also be horses who are considered too valuable to turn out with a companion, though you have to consider whether a horse would be more stressed and at risk of injury through being isolated than if turned out with a quiet, unshod companion.

Studs, even those breeding valuable potential racehorses, usually turn out in compatible groups – though obviously they make an exception for stallions, and top studs have special stallion paddocks with extra high fencing and turn out stallions alone. Broodmares settle amicably once they have worked out a pecking order, and colts and fillies are in groups arranged according to gender and age.

A quiet, amenable pony or elderly gelding is an asset on any yard and one of my children's ponies played this role for many years. Such an animal can become a friend for a single nervous or vulnerable horse when circumstances demand. He will be a calming influence on a volatile companion, give confidence to a nervous one and generally be worth his weight in gold.

KEY POINTS

- Whether regarded primarily as a food source or a turnout area, grassland must be well maintained.

- Specialist knowledge of your type of land is essential – general guidelines are useful, but don't work across the board.

- Grassland sown for cattle has a higher food value, so your horse management must take this into account.

- Stay observant to keep horses at grass safe.

- The most essential pasture management task is to remove droppings as often as possible.

CHAPTER 4

School Time

An arena comes high on most owners' list of essentials and I couldn't function without mine. I use it daily for schooling on the flat and over fences, lungeing and teaching clients on their own horses. I don't have an indoor school, but do hire one in the run-up to big indoor shows so that my horses get used to working in this environment.

WHERE TO SCHOOL

Although I wouldn't be without my arena, I also feel strongly that horses shouldn't always be worked within the confines of an indoor or outdoor school. Ours all hack out regularly, because we are lucky enough to have access to tracks and quiet roads. If the location of your yard means that you have to ride on roads which are dangerously busy then, unfortunately, you probably have to box up and head out to safer surroundings. This takes time and effort, but offers the extra advantage of getting inexperienced horses used to loading, travelling and unloading. It's well worth doing this; some people maintain that if a horse gets daily turnout, it doesn't matter if he is worked only in an arena, but I think most horses benefit from wider working horizons.

For the same reason, l also like to work horses in an open field when the going is suitable. It teaches them to adapt to different surroundings and terrain and, unless you are a dressage rider who only competes on artificial surfaces, your horse will sometimes have to perform on grass.

◀ It's beneficial to work horses in an open field when the going is suitable.

In practical terms, some horses are more forward-going – and hopefully, more responsive – out hacking and when schooling in a field than when working in an arena. This reminds us that when we school and compete, we want quick reactions to light aids and that it's possible to get them! It also helps teach a horse to respond when he is out of a rider's safety zone.

In most cases, there is also a psychological benefit. How many times do you hear riders say that their horses school beautifully at home but become distracted at competitions? Getting them out and about is part of the acclimatisation process and 'thinking outside the school' can help. It will also help you, by giving you confidence that you and your horse can work well outside the comfort zone.

Are some horses too valuable to be hacked out or worked on less-than-perfect going? Everyone has to make a choice, but some of our most enlightened and successful riders in all spheres make sure their horses are ridden out regularly.

Don't be blinkered into assuming that any schooling area is better than nothing. One which provides uneven going, or has a surface unsuitable for the work your horse is doing, could compromise your horse's soundness.

SCHOOL HOMEWORK

If you want to build an arena, you will probably need planning permission, whether it is for private or commercial use. Arena installation is never going to be cheap, but mistakes can be even more expensive. Even if you have access to machinery such as earth-moving equipment, consult specialist arena builders rather than assuming that you can save money by doing all or part of the work yourself.

This can be important at the planning stage. Although arena construction companies, like those who construct stable buildings, are unlikely to get involved in individual planning applications, they should be able to provide photographs of similar projects to show what the finished arena will look like.

Established companies should be able to provide testimonials, but you should also ask whether they have built for clients in your area who would talk to you about their experience and perhaps let you visit and see the arena in use. Do your own research, too. Ask others who they chose to build their arenas, what surface they opted for, how they overcame any problems and if, in hindsight, there is anything they wished they had or hadn't done.

There are several factors to consider when siting an arena and it's best to ask the companies you are considering to make a site visit. Many will do this without charging.

If you have a choice of sites, do you want your arena to be in quiet surroundings, or where horses who are being worked can see the yard and other things going on? This comes down to personal preference: some riders believe that horses should be free from distractions in a learning environment and others feel that an arena in busier surroundings replicates a competition environment and that horses should get used to this from the start.

My school is surrounded by fields used for grazing, so there may be times when a horse is asked to work despite the fact that others are eating or even charging around in the field behind the surrounding post and rails and hedging. It is sited close to the stables, so some horses are able to watch what is going on. As discussed in Chapter 2, some horses enjoy this whilst others prefer a quieter environment.

Bringing in materials means that access for large lorries is needed. If your arena site demands that access be made through fields, you may have to wait for decent weather conditions to minimise damage.

Good drainage is vital to the functionality of an arena and although preparing the base and sorting out drainage will eat up a large chunk of your budget, it's false economy to skimp at this stage. The right surface is important, but if you don't get your arena right from the ground up, nothing can work miracles.

There are different types of base available and you need to talk to your contractor about considerations such as budget, the amount of use the arena will be given and even prevalent weather conditions. Fencing is another consideration. In some circumstances, owners may choose not to have exterior fencing. This cuts down overall costs and some dressage riders believe they get a truer picture

of the way horses work when there are no barriers. However, this is a minority view. The danger of doing without arena fencing is that accidents happen and every rider parts company with a horse at some time. Good arena fencing makes it much more likely that a horse will stay within its confines and is very much a safety measure when working with young or inexperienced animals. It also means that you can loose-school a horse in your arena, though I use a circular pen for this.

Post and rail is the favourite choice for arena fencing, but there are other options. Depending on the lie of the land, your arena contractors may suggest building an earth embankment – though for extra security, you may still want to have post and rail.

SIZE MATTERS

Research shows that horses worked in large outdoor arenas, particularly when the main focus is on jumping, are less prone to injury than those worked in small indoor ones. So if you're thinking of installing an arena and will be doing a lot of jumping, try to budget for a larger one, if possible. If you're sticking to dressage dimensions, you'll find that building a 60 × 20m arena rather than a 40 × 20m one doesn't add as much to your overall bill as you might think.

If you want to jump in your arena, the minimum size usually recommended is 60 × 25m. Guidelines for circular pens for lungeing or loose work are a minimum of 15m diameter, though most trainers prefer them to be at least 20m diameter. Mine is 30m diameter and I have found it invaluable for loose-schooling, which is part of all my horses' regime, and for backing youngsters.

I've never had a horse who doesn't enjoy working in it and it enables me to see him moving without any interference. It also enables me to see if he is naturally more supple on one rein than another – most are – so I can tailor a lungeing and schooling regime to help him become equally supple on both reins.

Having a 30m pen means I can set up a single jump and use poles on the ground set at distances for trot or canter. Working on a curve means that the horse has to think more about where he puts his feet than when negotiating poles on a straight line, but because he is loose and not restricted by a lunge line, he also finds it easier to adjust his balance.

In recent years, I've been able to refurbish our original school and now have the luxury of two. One is a 40 × 20m and I prefer this one for working green horses or ones I suspect might be difficult. Horses have enough room to go forward, but are also contained and kept on the turn more easily. Both horses and riders seem to find a psychological security when working in this smaller one. However, when it is necessary to work two or three horses at the same time, a larger arena offers obvious advantages. When horses are warming up at competitions, they have to work with others. They can find this exciting or frightening and, bearing in mind that not all other riders are that savvy and considerate when warming up in company, it is safe practice to accustom horses to working in company at home. It also teaches riders to be able to concentrate on what they and their horses are doing, but be able to keep out of each other's way.

SCHOOL SCIENCE

There has been a lot of research into what makes a good arena. Most has focused on surfaces and researchers say that there is no perfect surface for every job. Dressage horses need to work on a surface that provides stability and confidence, whilst showjumpers need these qualities plus a small amount of 'cut' as they land over a fence. A top-level Western reining horse has unique requirements, because when performing sliding stops and spins he needs to be able to slide through the surface.

Over the years, I've had three types of surface on my schools. The first was a mix of sand and fibres and we then switched to rubber chips with silica sand on top, hoping for better going in wet weather. Our current surface is a gel-coated one. Purists will point out that silica is a common constituent of sand in most settings, but it is a term used by arena manufacturers to denote sand that is washed and graded, as opposed to builders' sand.

Whatever surface you choose, keep it at the correct depth. Top-up requirements vary, depending on the surface and the amount of use an arena gets.

The Animal Health Trust, which carried out research into construction, use and maintenance of arena surfaces, has recommended points we should consider when building, maintaining and using arenas:

Construction

- Do use a solid base that drains well, such as hard limestone, under the riding surface.

- Do make the base of the arena level or with a slight incline (1/100) to assist with drainage.

- Do use the same base under the whole arena, especially if adding an extension.

- Do ensure that your arena drains adequately and evenly.

- Do choose an appropriate surface for the type of riding you are doing: for example, jumping and dressage need a more stable surface than Western reining.

- Do choose a surface that can cope with the number of horses working on it between reasonable levelling or maintenance intervals.

- Do use a surface that you can keep even across the arena.

- Do use a surface that you have the equipment and time to maintain properly.

- Do choose a surface suitable for the weather conditions of the arena location.

- Do choose a surface that keeps the same moisture content in dry conditions, even if the actual moisture content has to be achieved by watering.

- Do choose an outdoor surface that does not change dramatically in varying conditions.

■ Do be careful selecting the type of sand for your arena: use small angular grain (fine) sand for a more stable surface than large round grains of coarse sand, which can give a deep and unstable surface.

■ Do use a layer of rubber over sand if you can, as this helps keep the sand moist and the arena more even.

■ Do add fibre to a sand-based arena, as this can make it more stable.

■ Do remember that whilst adding wax to a sand surface may help maintain moisture content, it needs to be suitable for the temperature range of the arena location.

■ Don't ride in arenas where the surface is hard or very deep, if avoidable.

■ Don't ride in arenas where the surface is uneven, if avoidable.

Maintenance

■ Do level, harrow and/or roll your arena frequently using the appropriate type of equipment for the surface. Follow manufacturers' guidelines but, depending on the type of surface and type of riding, an arena is likely to benefit from at least daily maintenance if approximately twenty horses are using it per day. The more horses use an arena, the more often it will need to be maintained.

■ Do make sure that all parts of the arena ride in the same way and that corners do not get deep and unstable. Make the entire arena surface uniform by harrowing and rolling each area as necessary.

■ Do move jumps around in the arena so that different areas get worked at different times.

■ Do use the appropriate type of maintenance for different types of arena surface. For example, a sand surface that becomes deep and unstable may need frequent watering and rolling. A wax-coated surface that becomes hard or with hills and troughs may need deep harrowing.

■ Do use appropriate types of maintenance and surface for different types of sports. Do maintain the arena more frequently when it is used for lungeing.

■ Do water a sand-based arena if it becomes dry and deep.

■ Use a watering system that dampens the surface evenly. Don't water in patches so that you get areas of puddles and dryness, as this will increase the risk of your horse slipping and tripping.

Riding

- Do ride all over the arena to help your horse's co-ordination and balanced fitness.

- Don't just ride on the outside track, as it makes the arena surface uneven and increases the risk of problems.

- Don't always lunge in the same part of the arena.

- Do ride outdoors as much as possible to promote respiratory health.

- Do ride your horse on a variety of different surfaces (artificial arena surfaces, grass, tracks, tarmac) but don't work your horse hard or fast on a surface that he is not used to.

- Do train your horse on the same surface type you compete on.

- Avoid riding on an uneven or patchy surface, as your horse can lose his balance moving suddenly from one area to another, or struggle in deep corners.

- Don't work your horse hard or for long on a deep or slippery surface.

TAKING CARE

Correct maintenance is as important as correct construction and a 'perfect' surface that is poorly maintained may be more detrimental to a horse's soundness and performance than one which is not ideal, but well looked after. One of the simplest but most important rules is to pick up droppings before they become trampled into the surface. People often don't realise the extent to which trampled droppings can compromise drainage.

The heavier the use an arena is put to, the more frequently the surface will need to be levelled. Regular levelling will minimise the risk of horses tripping or stumbling. If your arena incorporates a membrane, this will also minimise the risk of it being damaged. This can happen if the surface becomes too thin in certain areas.

An arena leveller is a great investment and there are designs that can be used with quads and 4wd vehicles as well as tractors. Check that the model you consider is suitable for your surface and look for designs that bring in material from the kickboards.

You may also want to think about a watering system to keep dust levels down, particularly if you have an indoor school. These range from fully automatic systems to travelling and manual sprinklers.

A NEW LOOK

If you're looking to rejuvenate an arena that isn't riding as well as you'd like, talk to a specialist company. The latest mixer products can make a big difference.

Good lighting can give you double the use of your arena, especially in winter. Most people need specialist help to ensure that light coverage is even and that lights are set at the right height and in the best positions. Things to take into account include the eye level of a rider – typically 2m–2.5m above ground level, but obviously higher when jumping – and siting lights to give uniform light whilst avoiding glare and shadows.

Arena mirrors are becoming increasingly popular, especially with dressage riders. They must be made from safety glass and some types can be moved up or down and put in portrait or landscape position.

◀ Arena mirrors are becoming increasingly popular and allow riders to check their position and confirm a horse's way of going.

KEY POINTS

- Check planning requirements.

- Getting specialist advice from the start will pay dividends.

- If you have a specialist yard, choose a surface suitable for the work your horses will be doing.

- The base construction is just as important as the surface.

- A good drainage system will extend the life of your arena and enable you to use it for all or most of the year.

- Think big when jumping or when you want to work several horses at the same time – a larger arena is better for your horse, more versatile and may not be as expensive as you think compared to the cost of a smaller one.

- Once you've made your investment, look after it. Maintenance is vital and one of the most important tasks is to remove droppings before they are trodden into the surface.

- Choose an arena leveller suitable for your surface.

- A watering system may be needed to keep down dust in dry periods in an indoor school.

- A lighting system extends your riding time, but lights must be sited correctly to give uniform light without glare and shadows.

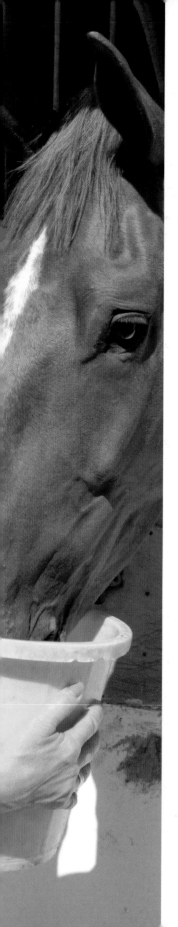

CHAPTER 5

Feeding

Correct feeding is vital for a horse's well-being and for helping him achieve optimum performance. Today, we know far more about the science of equine nutrition than ever before. There may be times when that seems like a mixed blessing, but if you want to know how best to care for your horse, you need to keep in touch with research and scientific discoveries.

That doesn't mean we need to set up a lab next to the tack room; rather, we all need to be aware of the latest thinking and evaluate how it applies to our horses. Knowing your horse and gauging how he feels, as well as how he looks, is as important in deciding how to feed him as it is in deciding how to work him.

Owners also need to be able to tell the difference between science and clever marketing. Walk into any feed shop or click on any website and you'll find hundreds of feed products, from basic horse and pony cubes to supplements. Deciding what to feed your horse – and what he doesn't need – may seem confusing, but the key is to bring it back to basics and let science help you, not cause confusion.

Horses have different nutritional requirements at different stages of life. For instance, those of a growing youngster will differ from those of a veteran or broodmare – and there will be differences between animals of the same age. A 2-year-old native pony should not be fed the same as a 2-year-old TB in a racing yard! Get advice from an equine vet or qualified nutritionist on how to meet individual requirements whilst following good general principles of feeding.

Look at feeding as part of your overall management programme, not in isolation. Feeding the best-quality forage and feed won't compensate for poor dental health or a heavy worm burden.

EATING LIKE A HORSE

Telling someone they 'eat like a horse' is usually a euphemism for accusing them of greed. Given the chance, horses will spend most of their time eating, but that's what nature intends.

▲ Horses have different nutritional requirements at different stages of life.

Where we must be careful is that the horse has evolved to eat forage; moreover, forage of lower nutritional value than that which a lot of modern grazing provides. To keep his digestive system healthy and to help keep him happy, we must allow him to follow a natural eating pattern.

Two things complicate this. One is that feral horses might travel long distances in the search for food, whilst domesticated horses obviously don't. However, the latter do have to work. In many cases, they may need nothing more than grass, hay or haylage and a supply of vitamins and minerals to make up any shortcomings. In others, they will need extra fuel.

The other complication is that whilst feral equines are not overweight, domesticated ones often are. Some researchers say that half the UK's equine population could be obese. This means that all owners should know how to assess their horses' condition and how to establish and maintain an animal's correct weight without compromising other aspects of his well-being. No pressure, then!

▶ Feral ponies travel long distances in search of food.

WEIGHTY MATTERS

Looking at a horse you don't know and deciding whether he is just right, too fat or too thin is relatively easy, as long as you can tell the difference between a fit horse and a thin one – more of that later in this chapter. Some owners find that, if they see a horse every day, it can be difficult to tell purely by eye whether he is gradually losing or gaining weight until it becomes glaringly obvious.

The best strategy is to use a scoring system, known as condition scoring or body fat scoring, together with a weigh tape or, if you're lucky, a weighbridge. Condition scoring is a twofold technique, as you need to feel for fat deposits as well as making a visual assessment. Horses store fat on their neck and topline, over their shoulders, on their ribs, spine, backbone and pelvic area and at the top of the tail.

Follow the guidelines below; the best way is to look at your horse from the side, divide him into three sections, score each area and divide the total by three to give an average. Do this every two weeks, so you don't miss those gradual changes.

Record your horse's weight at similar intervals. Anyone can use a weigh tape, but be careful to position it according to the instructions and try to use it at the same time each day, in similar circumstances. A horse who has been grazing all day will be more 'blown out' than one who has been stabled overnight.

A weigh tape won't give as accurate a reading as a weighbridge, but will tell you whether your horse is maintaining, gaining or losing weight and will also help you to work out accurate dosage rates for wormers. Do take any opportunity to use a weighbridge, if only for the sake of interest. Most equine veterinary clinics have weighbridges and some feed companies have ones which they will take to large yards and shows.

Taking photographs regularly also helps, as it gives you a visual record. The photos opposite show a Riding Club cob who was overweight on purchase and gradually lost 63kg (nearly 140lb) – more than the weight of his rider and tack combined.

Be realistic, but don't make excuses. A cob is never going to have the same definition as a Thoroughbred event horse, but he can still be in good condition. At the same time, you don't have to beat yourself up because you can't feel a cob's ribs without gentle pressure – though you shouldn't need to poke through lots of blubber.

▼ Weigh tapes are valuable when positioned and used correctly.

Don't make the common mistake of assuming that you can turn fat into muscle. It's a physiological impossibility, but there are still people who think that a horse needs to carry extra weight before he can be got fit. Nor, of course, should you try to work a horse hard when he is in poor condition because you think he won't be able to misbehave!

▲ Before and after: *left* this Riding Club cob was obese on arrival at his new owner's yard. *right* He eventually lost more than the weight of his rider.

Winning scores

Scores can be made either from 0–5, including half marks, or 0–9. Welfare organisations and feed companies provide online advice and videos, but here are guidelines for the 0–5 method.

0 = Very poor, emaciated The rump is sunken, with a deep cavity under the tail. Backbone, ribs and pelvis are prominent and the horse will appear to have a ewe (upside down) neck when this may not (skeletally) be the case.

1 = Poor As above, but to a lesser extent.

2 = Moderate The neck is firm but narrow and the rump is flat either side of the spine, though the spine itself is not visible. Ribs may be visible, but not markedly so as in 1 and 2.

3 = Good The ribs can be felt but are covered, the rump is rounded and the neck is firm, but not cresty.

4 = Fat There is a gutter along the back and pelvis and it's very difficult to feel the ribs.

5 = Obese The gutter along the back and pelvis is deep and you can't feel the ribs. There are pads of fat on the crest and/or neck and/or shoulders.

PLAYING THE NUMBERS GAME

The first question every owner asks is: how much does my horse need? Nutritionists say that, in terms of quantity, the average daily intake should be 2–2.5 per cent of the horse's weight, so a horse weighing 500kg (1,100lb) who does not need to lose weight would need 10–12.5kg (22–27.5lb). If he needs to lose weight, it's better to feed at the 2 per cent level unless your vet tells you otherwise, and to reduce the energy level of his diet so you are giving him fewer calories. Calories are simply a measure of energy, so reducing energy levels doesn't mean you are altering his enthusiasm for and ability to work to a normal level. As an example, if you are feeding horse and pony cubes formulated for a horse in all-round work, switch to lower-energy high-fibre cubes.

The next consideration is how to work out the ratio of hard feed – if applicable – to forage. Forage levels should provide at least 60 per cent of the diet and, for most horses, will account for 80–100 per cent. The more you cut the forage levels, the greater the risk of digestive problems and stomach ulcers.

GRAZING TACTICS

Talking numbers is one thing, but factoring in the nutritional value of grazing and how much grass your horse eats is another. Standard advice is that grass is more nutritious in spring and summer, but you must also consider environmental conditions. Grass will only stop growing when the *soil temperature*, not the air temperature, falls below 5 °C (41 °F), or during periods of drought, so periods of mild weather and average rainfall late in the year will mean it continues to grow.

It's impossible to give a definitive guide on how much grass a horse will take in, because availability, grass length and how fast a horse eats all affect intake. Also, feed values vary between grass types and even between the same grass species in different locations in different climatic conditions. Studies show that the average intake is around 1kg (2.2lb) per hour. One research project found that restricting turnout time didn't have as much of an effect on intake as was thought: ponies used in the study learned that they had reduced eating time and grazed continually, rather than having rest breaks. That said, there are some horses and ponies who never seem to stop eating even when turned out all the time.

Sometimes, it's essential to restrict grass intake. We don't want horses to become obese, nor do we want to increase the risk of laminitis for susceptible animals (see Chapter 10.) The answer is to strip-graze or use a grazing muzzle.

Strip-grazing, either by fencing off a small area or using a round pen, restricts a horse's range of movement, as he doesn't have enough space to gallop and let

off steam. This in itself may be a problem if you don't or can't ensure that he has adequate exercise. If you need to limit movement on veterinary advice, a round pen is safer.

Grazing muzzles are said to reduce grass intake by up to a third, but must be fitted carefully to avoid rubs and must never prevent the horse from drinking. There are two main designs in common use, though detailed features vary from manufacturer to manufacturer. One is bucket-shaped with a hole in the bottom; the other resembles a plastic tray with high sides and attaches to a specially designed headcollar. All grazing muzzles must have a breakaway point, so if the wearer manages to get the muzzle caught up, it will release.

Most horses accept grazing muzzles, though you need to keep watch after introducing one to ensure that your horse isn't one of the few who has a tantrum. He will probably take a little time to get used to it and realise that he can graze, but don't relent and take it off after a few minutes if he stands and looks at you in a pathetic fashion! Put it on in a quiet but matter of fact way, but don't bump it against his muzzle. Some horses accept a muzzle more easily if you place a sliver of apple or carrot in the bottom.

Unfortunately, despite what manufacturers, say there are a few animals who refuse to accept grazing muzzles and become stressed even when allowed time to acclimatise. In these cases, your only option will be to strip-graze.

▲ *left* Strip-grazing is a useful strategy when trying to keep a horse's weight down.

▲ *right* Grazing a horse in a round pen helps when trying to limit food intake.

▶ Grazing muzzles give the benefit of turnout whilst restricting the amount of grass a horse can eat.

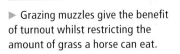

FORAGE

Good-quality forage is a vital element of any horse's or pony's diet and whilst we all have budgets to work to, I never begrudge paying a realistic price for good hay and, when needed, haylage. Hay is always my first choice, because it has a much higher fibre content, but haylage may be needed for horses with dust-related respiratory problems if soaking or steaming hay is not enough.

When buying haylage, look for a product that has at least 55 per cent but no more than 70 per cent dry matter. Some owners will want to have hay or haylage analysed. A typical analysis will tell you:

– Dry matter level – particularly important with haylage, as the higher the water content, the lower the fibre level.

– Crude protein level – calculated from the nitrogen content.

– Basic or comprehensive mineral analysis depending on requirements.

– Hygiene – measures moulds and yeasts.

▲ Good-quality hay is always my first choice of forage and I will have it analysed, mainly to assess the protein level.

Commercial haylage from a big manufacturer – which usually means the bagged rather than wrapped variety – will have an analysis printed on the bag.

We have our hay analysed, mainly because we find it helpful to know the protein level. However, I also judge it on cleanliness and smell. If you opt for hay analysis, then in theory you will need to have every batch tested.

One study says that up to 80 per cent of horses are affected by some degree of recurrent airway obstruction (RAO), previously referred to as chronic obstructive pulmonary disease (COPD). Another points to RAO affecting half the number of horses who are stabled. In both cases, sufferers identified ranged from horses who showed no obvious symptoms to those who were severely affected. As environment – including stable design and bedding – as well as forage has a huge effect on respiratory health, you can't blame hay alone. At the same time, this shows the importance of choosing and preparing forage correctly.

I find that, with many horses, I don't need to soak top-quality hay, though I know some authorities will not agree. Other horses need hay either soaked or steamed and we use a commercial hay steamer. Steaming is more hygienic and preserves the nutrient quality better than soaking, though practical issues and finance – you need a power supply, and commercial steamers aren't cheap – mean that some owners will continue to soak.

When soaking, hay should always be soaked in clean water and should be completely submerged. Soak for about half an hour if you want to retain the nutrient quality. Nutritionists advise that soaking for an hour or more means that you reduce energy levels – which, of course, can be a useful strategy when you need a horse to lose weight.

In theory, you can steam hay by putting a full haynet in a metal dustbin, pouring on one or more kettles of boiling water, replacing the lid tightly and leaving the steam to disperse. In practice, this will not do as thorough or as hygienic a job as a purpose-made steamer. It is also time-consuming, so not practical on large yards. Some resourceful owners make their own steaming units by combining steamers designed for removing wallpaper with suitable containers, though equine industry manufacturers say this does not give the same level of hygiene.

Haylage does not need soaking, nor will it lose nutrient quality: once the bag or wrappings are opened, it is fed too quickly for nutrient levels to fall. Its main disadvantage is that the protective wrapping material is easily pierced; it may only take one bird to decide to peck at it to break the sealed environment, resulting in mould developing.

Any bales showing mould patches must be discarded and a good supplier will replace them as long as you keep them to prove your claim, but it does cause inconvenience. It's bad enough when haylage is delivered, but even worse for one-horse owners who lack storage space and collect three or four small bales at a time from a local feed supplier.

There have been rare incidents of horses dying or becoming extremely ill because of botulism – caused by bacteria in soil – in haylage. This can happen if the grass is cut too close to the ground so that small amounts of soil are also baled. However, reputable manufacturers and suppliers of haylage made especially for equines will be well aware of this.

Silage should *never* be fed to horses. Worryingly, this is sometimes still recommended as a safe practice. It isn't – there is a considerable risk that silage will contain the bacteria responsible for botulism. In any case, its protein content is too high for horses.

Whether you opt for hay or haylage, choose a type suitable for the individual horse. Hay ranges from lucerne hay made from alfalfa (which is like rocket fuel in a bale but may be suitable for horses in true hard work, such as racehorses and fully fit event horses), to hay that is suitable for good doers.

WATER WORKS

The other essential in your horse's diet is, of course, water, yet it's something owners often pay little attention to. If your horse isn't hydrated, his welfare is compromised and so is your safety. A dehydrated horse – or human – can't function properly, but there's more to it than making sure that his water buckets are full, or that the automatic watering system is working properly.

As well as providing a constant supply of clean, fresh water, you have to ensure that your horse is drinking enough. As mentioned in Chapter 2, I don't use automatic waterers, as most systems don't allow you to monitor how much a horse drinks. I wouldn't even use a system with gauges, as I've seen too many cases where horses have damaged pipes, or systems have become blocked.

By using buckets or corner mangers as water containers, you can ensure that your horse feels safe to drink. I never use mangers that hook on to doors, as there is too much potential for accidents to happen. Those who like to eat and drink in private prefer buckets at the back of their stable. Setting buckets in old tyres prevents them from being kicked over, but you must remove buckets and scrub them out daily, not just take in fresh supplies to refill them.

I've also found that horses vary in their temperature preferences. Some will always drink when offered cold water, whilst others prefer it when the chill is taken off – which, confusingly, is what the old grooms used to call 'chilled water'. This might sound pernickety, but it's attention to detail that will help keep your horse healthy.

Watch out for the quality of your horse's water in the field, too. Textbooks often say that troughs should be sited away from trees to minimise leaves falling in, but that's easier said than done. However, they should be checked daily and cleaned out regularly and, in freezing conditions, you need to break the ice frequently. Floating a ball in a trough doesn't work, but Canadian friends tell me they use insulated and very expensive troughs.

PRINCIPLES OF FEEDING

There's an old saying that 'The eye of the master makes the horse fat.' This doesn't mean, as is sometimes suggested, that in the days when wealthy owners had full-time grooms they needed to keep a close eye on what they were feeding to make sure they weren't stealing and selling oats and other feedstuffs. Rather, it means that you need to keep a close eye on your horse's condition and feed him as an individual.

Knowing your horse and monitoring his condition is still important. Other considerations to take into account are his age, type and workload. For instance, growing youngstock have different nutritional requirements from mature horses and, as we've already seen, a TB racehorse in really hard work or one peaking in fitness for a top-level horse trials will have a different diet from that of a horse who hacks out most of the time.

We'll look at special needs later in this chapter but, as most readers will be working out how to feed a horse who is ridden regularly, you also need to define how hard he works. Nutritionists say that many owners get the answer wrong, as they misinterpret their horses' workload and think they are working much harder than is the case.

Generally accepted definitions, related to specific disciplines, are:

Maintenance – animals who are not working.

Light work – applies to most horses and ponies. It includes hacking, schooling three or four times a week when most of the work is done in walk and trot, and horses who compete in low-level competition in any discipline, such as Preliminary dressage, showjumping over small courses and endurance/pleasure rides up to 30km (19 miles).

Medium work – is usually defined as competition and associated preparatory work which has gone up a gear. This includes more demanding schooling, including regular jumping and competing at affiliated level most weekends.

Hard work – is a category that very few horses come into. We're talking about top-level competition – Advanced dressage, top-level showjumping, eventing at 3* and 4* level and racing. Horses who are hunting hard two or three times a week will probably come into this category, but they will be in a minority in the hunting field.

A horse's breed or type usually makes a difference to the way his diet needs to be planned. Cob type and native ponies, who have evolved to live on sparse grazing, are notoriously good doers and their owners often say that they get fat on fresh air. Conversely, many owners of TBs find it hard to keep weight on them through the winter. However, there are exceptions. If you have a pony or cob who is naturally forward-going and gets plenty of work, you might be one of the lucky owners who doesn't have to worry about him becoming obese. Similarly, there are TBs who are so laid-back they are horizontal and maintain weight easily.

ADDING EXTRA FUEL

There are a lot of ponies – and horses – who are good doers and work well and happily on a diet of good-quality forage. The only extras they will all need are a broad-spectrum vitamin and mineral supplement or low-calorie balancer to compensate for any deficiencies in the diet, and salt.

Others, including elderly retired animals who have lost teeth and can't chew properly, will need what can loosely be termed bucket feeds. This can range from short-chopped, high-fibre feed to cubes or mixes of appropriate nutritional value. In extreme cases, you may need to feed cubes which have been soaked in water to make a soft mash.

The easiest horse to feed is the mature horse following a regular work routine, who has no health or behavioural issues. Follow the rule of maintaining a high ratio of forage to hard feed and, if he doesn't maintain appropriate condition, add a feed appropriate for his type, workload and temperament.

Choosing commercial feeds may seem complicated when you see how many brands and how many products are available, but it doesn't have to be. Deciding which brand to buy is personal choice and there are many well-known and established names. In the end, it may come down to availability and price.

Visitors to my yard are often surprised when they discover that we have just four types of feed in our feed room – low-energy cubes, low-energy mix, chaff and non-molassed, quick-soak sugar beet – and we manage to feed a wide range of horses and ponies successfully. Most are doing the same job – showing – but they vary from TB show hacks to Irish sport horses and cobs. We also have horses in for breaking and schooling, who may or may not be intended for, or from, the showing world. There have been times when we have had racehorses, event horses, mountain and moorland ponies, show horses and youngsters in for backing and, with the exception of racehorses and event horses at peak fitness, we have never had to extend our feed range. Even then, some horses event on hard feed with a lower energy level than you would assume their job demanded.

I always include chaff, because it is high in fibre and slows down the eating rate. I prefer chaff with a reasonably high oil content, because oil is a great form of slow-release energy and helps promote a healthy coat, skin and hooves. If a horse is on a weight-loss regime, I'll use chaff with a low oil content. It's hard to find chaff without some form of coating, as this application minimises dust levels, but if you're cutting your horse's calories, avoid those with heavy levels of molasses.

At one time, I didn't feed sugar beet, because it was time-consuming to prepare when feeding lots of horses and I was worried about it fermenting and causing digestive problems. I now feed quick-soak sugar beet, as it is high in fibre, tempts 'picky' eaters and helps keep horses hydrated. I believe that feeds with high sugar levels can affect behaviour, though I know this goes against the advice of some nutritionists. However, the name sugar beet is misleading, as pellets and shreds for equine consumption are made from what is left over after sugar has been extracted from the root crop. It is the molasses coating, added to try to make it more palatable, which boosts sugar content: feed the unmolassed type and you solve the problem.

The argument put forward against the theory that sugar can affect a horse is that grass has high sugar levels and that it is the overall extra energy level that tips the balance, rather than sugar itself. However, my own experience and that of others has convinced me otherwise, which is why I also avoid molassed feeds if possible.

COMPOUNDS AND CONCENTRATES

Cubes are usually cheaper than mixes, as they are cheaper to make. Don't fall into the trap of thinking that because mixes look more appetising, your horse is bound to find them more enjoyable. They might look more interesting to us, but give a horse the choice and he'll eat grass all day without becoming bored. The fact that mixes look like muesli is more of a marketing tactic than a nutritional advantage: companies hope that because mixes appeal visually to owners, we'll think they'll appeal to horses more than boring brown cubes. Having said that, you will occasionally find a horse who eats mixes more readily than cubes.

If you're not sure which type of feed to buy for a particular horse, feed company nutritionists will give free advice, albeit based on their own range. An independent, registered equine nutritionist should be totally unbiased, but will naturally charge for advice.

The advantage of feeding a compound feed – or concentrates, if you prefer the term – is that it will be nutritionally balanced and each batch will have the same value; unless the formulation is changed, 1kg (2.2lb) of a company's horse and pony cubes will have the same feed value as that from a bag you bought the previous year. However, whilst the names put on feed bags may be the same, the nutritional value may vary – for example, one company's formulation of a high-fibre, horse and pony or competition feed may have different nutrient levels from another's. This means you need to know how to read a feed bag label.

There is a statutory statement which includes things such as the name of the feed, indicating the type of animal it is meant for; whether it is a complete feed or – as in most cases – designed to be fed as a sole concentrate source alongside forage; the name and address of the manufacturer; bag weight; best before date and date of manufacture.

You will also find details of the feed's nutrient analysis. By law, manufacturers only have to declare crude protein, crude fibre, oil, ash, copper and vitamins A, D and E, though some give more information. Don't be confused by the mention of ash: it refers to the mineral value, determined by burning the feed to leave a mineral residue.

If you change from one feed to another, do it gradually. Sudden changes cause digestive upsets, so mix a little of the new feed in with the old and alter the proportions over the space of a few days. Ideally, apply the same principle to forage: mix a little of a new batch of hay with the old and gradually switch from one to the other.

The accepted principle of making changes gradually means that the once traditional practice of giving a horse a bran mash once a week doesn't make sense. It goes back to the time when horses worked hard all week and were given Sundays off – not for their own sake, but because Sunday was supposedly a day of rest. The thinking was that a bran mash given on a Saturday night had a laxative effect and cleared out a horse's system, but we now know that isn't true.

FEEDING INTERVALS AND ROUTINE

Feeding intervals depend on the routine you're able to establish and whether your horse is a ready eater. I feed 'bucket feeds' twice a day, because when my horses are stabled they have plenty of forage and so don't go for long periods without fibre passing through their digestive systems. Others, especially those whose horses are in such hard work they need larger quantities of hard feed, will feed three or four times a day.

Whatever you decide, don't feed more than 2kg (4.4lb) dry weight of hard feed in one meal. Your horse may well eat it, but you'll be overloading his digestive system. If you're feeding more than 4kg (8.8lb) per day, you need to split it into three or more meals.

When you keep your own horses on your own yard, you have the freedom to establish a routine of feeding at consistent times of day. This is a practice that should be established by owners/managers of all full livery yards. If you keep a horse at DIY livery yard, you will probably have to fit in with yard rules and routines. As long as these follow good practice, that is the best way to keep horses happy.

Problems are more likely to arise when owners at DIY yards follow their own routines with no consideration for others. For example, if one person feeds their horse at 6 a.m. and others deliver their horses' breakfast at different times, you will have a yard of unhappy horses. The only way to get round this is to have agreed feeding times or for the first person on the yard to distribute all feeds.

FEED SUPPLEMENTATION

Need and suitability

The equine supplements market has become an industry in its own right and there are probably more horses who have extras in their diet than those who don't. Whether or not that's a good thing is open to debate; there are some excellent products out there, but there is also a lot of great marketing.

There are things you must check before using any type of commercial supplement.

If your horse has a problem, get veterinary advice first. Only a vet can make a diagnosis. For example, if a horse is showing signs of stiffness, don't assume that this is a result of osteoarthritis. This *may be* the case and you may find that a supplement designed to reduce stiffness will help, but there may be another reason; for instance, a horse who injures his back, neck or pelvis may hold himself awkwardly to try to relieve the discomfort.

Another scenario is that of the 'moody mare'. There are lots of supplements said to help, but if the cause is an ovarian cyst, nutrition is not the answer.

In the case of products intended to promote calmness, look at your horse's type, temperament and level of schooling and your own experience and confidence. A sensitive horse needs a sensitive rider and an inexperienced horse, particularly one who lacks confidence, needs a rider who can metaphorically hold his hand, give him confidence and explain things.

Here, you also need to look at your overall management. Does your horse get enough time in the field and enough exercise and work? There is a difference between exercise and work: exercise keeps him moving, but work also gives him things to think about. My horses, whatever their jobs, love pole work and gridwork tailored to their needs and level of training and any rider – even someone who doesn't want to jump – can use poles on the ground to improve a horse's balance, flexibility and interest.

Is his diet suitable for his needs? The obvious example is the horse on a high-energy feed when what he really needs is one that keeps him content, but has a lower energy level.

◀ Pole work adds variety to a horse's work even if you don't want to jump.

If you compete, is the supplement you intend to use competition-legal? FEI rules on prohibited and controlled substances are adopted by all disciplines' governing bodies and are a minefield. Keep an eye on the FEI list of prohibited substances, because it is updated regularly. If in doubt, check with your vet, but be aware that the ultimate responsibility rests with you.

Does a manufacturer list all the ingredients on the packaging? They should do, but some believe this gives others the opportunity to copy products and try to use general terms rather than specifics. Be careful, too, about withdrawal times on feedstuffs and medication (if you aren't sure about medication, check with your vet). Some ingredients and components remain in a horse's system for several days after the last administration and if your horse tests positive, no leeway will be given.

Are you sure that traces of the supplement – or medication – you add to a feed will only reach the horse it is intended for? Don't put it in a bucket of feed and take the bucket to the horse's manger: take the bucket of feed to the stable and then mix in whatever you need to add. Scrub out the bucket immediately afterwards and remove and scrub out the manger as soon as the horse has eaten. If you're on a big yard and someone puts a different horse in that stable, even if only for a few minutes, this avoids the risk of cross-contamination. The first thing any horse does when he enters a stable is investigate the manger.

Salt and electrolytes

Nutritionists agree that all horses need salt in their diet and the maintenance level for a horse who is resting or in light work is generally given as 25g (about 1oz) per day. That requirement increases as the workload goes up – or the horse sweats more – so get advice about an individual horse's needs. However, do not feed large amounts of salt without getting expert advice.

Compound feed contains salt, but not enough to satisfy a horse's requirement; the practical reason for this is apparently that if levels were higher, the moisture content would be too high because salt would attract it from the surrounding air and the paper feed sacks used by most companies would give way.

Some owners prefer to give horses free access to salt licks, believing that a horse will naturally take what he needs. Unfortunately, it doesn't work this way. Some horses will ignore a salt lick and some will become obsessed with it, so the only sure-fire method is to add what's needed to the feed.

Researchers now say that any horse doing more than light work needs electrolytes rather than salt alone. Electrolytes regulate how fluids are distributed throughout the body; the most important ones are sodium, potassium, chloride, calcium and magnesium. I use them regularly and know from my horses' performance that they are beneficial.

It has been reported that one litre of a horse's sweat contains about 3.5g sodium, 6g chloride, 1.2g potassium and 0.1g calcium. As a horse can easily lose five litres of sweat per hour when working at a moderate speed, this means he can lose around 50g electrolytes in that time. Low levels of electrolytes can contribute to poor performance and, in severe cases, to synchronous diaphragmatic flutter – colloquially known as 'the thumps' – where stimulation of the diaphragm leads to the chest twitching in time with the heartbeat.

It used to be thought that the best way to offer electrolytes was in drinking water and that horses should be offered plain water alongside it. Modern thinking is that they should be offered in feed or via a syringe in paste form, but with water available at all times.

Experts advise that electrolytes should be given every day, not just immediately before and during competition. The reason for this is that if you feed enough electrolytes during training, you will not need to increase the amount in the feed at competition time.

Vitamins and minerals

Is your horse getting the full spectrum of vitamins and minerals he needs? If you are feeding the recommended amount of a compound feed from a reputable company, the answer should be yes. However, there are some horses who either won't be getting compound feed or will be fed less than the recommended minimum amounts.

Feed company nutritionists say that if you can't feed the recommended minimum amount without your horse putting on too much weight, you should feed one with a lower energy level. That's logical, but doesn't help if you're already feeding a baseline energy level product.

Instead, you should feed an appropriate amount of either a broad-spectrum vitamin and mineral supplement or a feed balancer formulated for your horse's type and workload. Pelleted feed balancers, which are really concentrated compound feeds, pack essential nutrients into smaller quantities; they are usually fed at a rate of 500g (1.1lb) per day and usually have a more advanced formulation than many broad-spectrum supplements. I prefer them for this reason, and also because horses seem to find them more palatable.

Balancers can also be used to top-up nutrients, perhaps when a horse is a picky eater, but get advice from your feed company before doing this to ensure you don't cause an overload of micronutrients – essential elements that are needed only in very small amounts.

Probiotics

If your horse's digestive system is stressed, you may be advised to feed probiotics. These promote the health of beneficial micro-organisms which exist naturally in the gut. Independent registered nutritionist Clare MacLeod, author of *The Truth About Feeding Your Horse* (J. A. Allen), advises that a healthy horse on a high-fibre diet probably won't need them, but that they may be useful in the following scenarios:

- Older horses with impaired dental function.

- Situations where sudden changes in diet can't be avoided.

- After using antibiotics, wormers and some other drugs: ask your vet for advice.

- Stress linked to travel; moving home (temporarily or permanently).

- Stress linked to competition.

- Dehydration.

- Inadequate fibre in the diet – though this should be rectified.

- Weight loss or general failure to thrive, though veterinary advice should be sought in case there is an underlying cause not linked to stress.

- Illness, especially when accompanied by loss of appetite, digestive problems or infections.

Calmers

The most controversial but probably also the most widely used supplements are those formulated to promote calmness, colloquially known as calmers. They are controversial because there have been so few clinical trials, although there is anecdotal evidence in support of them.

One theory is that calmers work because administering them has a psychological effect on a rider: if you think something is going to produce a calmer horse, your anxiety will reduce, which will have a beneficial effect on your horse. A rider's demeanour definitely affects a horse; as the old saying goes, tension or fear goes down the rein into the horse's brain. However, I don't believe this is the only reason calmers can be useful and I've used a few competition-legal ones on horses who become anxious when coping with new experiences or particular circumstances.

Before using any type of calmer for competition, double-check the ingredients to make sure that they do not contravene rules on prohibited substances and be careful to avoid the risks of cross-contamination, as explained previously.

FEEDING FOR PURPOSE

As mentioned earlier, horses have different requirements at different stages of life and the best person to advise you on this is a qualified nutritionist. However, here are some general points.

Growing youngsters need nutrients for steady growth and development but you should still follow the principle that forage should make up most of the horse's diet and youngsters must not be allowed to become overweight. Too much weight puts strain on the limbs and internal organs and compromises a horse's future. In the worst cases, it may mean that he doesn't have one.

At the other end of the scale, horses generally have longer working lives than those of fifty years ago. Some of that is a result of advances in veterinary science, as we can identify, cure or manage conditions that would once have ended a horse's ability to work. However, animals in their late teens and above will still have issues that need to be managed, no matter how well they have been cared for. Age takes its toll, whether you are equine or human!

It's important to maintain any horse's dental health and this is crucial with an old horse. If he can't chew, he can't digest forage and feed properly. In some cases, feeding meadow (soft) hay or haylage may be enough, but your veteran may reach the stage where he can't chew either of these adequately. The next logical step is to give him a short-chop forage feed designed to be a hay replacer. Avoid molassed chaff, as it contains chopped straw – which your horse won't cope with – and the sugar levels will be too high when the chaff is fed in sufficient quantities.

Eventually, you may find that an old horse can't manage even short-chop feeds. Usually, the solution is to feed soaked high-fibre cubes and soaked sugar beet. As the horse's diet will then comprise bucket feeds, he must be fed at least three times a day, preferably more.

If your elderly horse is diagnosed with Cushing's syndrome (hyperadreno-corticism) he may suffer from glucose intolerance. He will also be at high risk of laminitis *all year round* and you must get specialist advice on how to feed him.

'Sharp' horses should, as always, be considered from every management angle – including that of whether the rider is up to dealing with a horse who needs a sensitive, balanced rider. Whilst it's important not to overfeed a sharp horse with too much high-energy feed, you also need to ensure that you don't make him irritable and at risk of developing stomach ulcers by cutting the quantity of his feed to an inappropriate level.

Often, the first advice given is 'cut his feed' when it should be 'give him an appropriate feed regime'. I've been sent horses for backing and schooling whose owners have cut out hard feed but not made sure that the horse has adequate good-quality forage and adequate nutrients. As a result, these poor horses have been hungry and miserable. When fed appropriate rations, which may or may not include a supplement designed to promote calmness, they have been happier and easier to deal with.

So-called lazy horses will not be changed into turbo-charged versions by feeding them racehorse cubes. Talk to a nutritionist about choosing the right feeding regime for your horse, but look at his levels of education, fitness and even motivation. A horse needs to be taught to go forward; he also needs to be fit enough to maintain his energy and to enjoy his work.

Correct feeding should be reflected by healthy hooves, skin and coat. Adding oil, a supplement with a high oil base, or cooked linseed to a horse's diet is often recommended as a way of encouraging a shiny coat, but if you struggle to keep your horse's weight down you have to remember that by adding these you are also adding calories.

Take extra care when looking after a horse or pony on box rest. Unless your vet advises otherwise, he needs appropriate ad lib forage and a broad-spectrum vitamin and mineral supplement or balancer. If he's a good doer who only gets that when he's working, soak hay for at least an hour to reduce energy levels and use a small mesh net to try to slow his eating rate. He should be able to have sliced carrots, apples and root vegetables and, if he has lost his appetite, these may help tempt him to eat. If he is the sort who loses condition quickly, you may be able to use a commercial feed formulated specifically for resting horses: as always, if you are in any doubt, ask your vet.

Be extra careful to get specialist advice when feeding broodmares at different stages of pregnancy, foals and breeding stallions during both the covering season and the 'off-season'. It's important to give them optimum levels of nutrients without allowing them to become overweight.

The only way for a horse – or human – to lose weight is through a combination of diet and exercise. As already discussed, you should think of feeding on a low-calorie basis at a daily rate of 2 per cent of the horse's weight and, if necessary, supplementing with extra nutrients. In some cases, it's appropriate to reduce the overall intake to 1.5 per cent, but only temporarily and only on advice from a vet or suitably qualified nutritionist.

FEED STORAGE AND HYGIENE

Hay and feed must be stored in a clean, dry environment. Bagged haylage can be stored in the open, if necessary.

Keep feed rooms, mangers and buckets clean and, if you mix feeds in buckets and tip them into mangers, ensure that each horse has his own easily identifiable bucket. This means that any supplements or medication reaches the right horse and avoids cross-contamination.

On a large yard, it makes sense for one person to mix the feeds even if others distribute them. I have a wipe-clean whiteboard in my feed room on which we write every horse's name, the type and quantity of feed he gets and any supplements or medication that need to be added. This helps efficiency and means that, if necessary, someone else can take charge of preparing feeds.

Keeping yards, storage buildings and feed rooms as clean and tidy as possible helps cut down the risk of vermin, though you can't always eliminate them. Nor can you ignore them: rats carry Weil's disease (Leptospirosis), which is a bacterial infection carried by animals. It is rare but possible for humans to develop it.

Many yards have yard cats to keep down vermin and there are charities which re-home feral cats to suitable environments. Most domestic cats are too well fed to earn their keep as rodent operatives!

▲ *left* Feed rooms, buckets and mangers must be kept clean.

▲ *right* I use a whiteboard on which I write every horse's name, the type and quantity of feed he gets and any supplements or medication which need to be added.

If the problem is so bad that you feel you need to use poison, remember that it is effective because it is palatable. Unfortunately, it is palatable to dogs and cats as well as to rats and mice, so be careful not to place it where animals other than those you are targeting have access. If necessary, call in a professional to deal with the problem.

Bird droppings are also a health hazard, but be aware that under the Wildlife and Countryside Act 1981 it is an offence to:

■ Intentionally kill, injure or take any wild bird.

■ Intentionally take, damage or destroy the nest of any wild bird whilst it is in use or being built.

■ Intentionally take or destroy the egg of any wild bird.

This legislation allows for some exceptions, such as pigeons, but get advice before taking action.

GOLDEN GUIDELINES

To sum up, the art and science of feeding is to understand feeding principles and how they are best applied to your individual horse. It always helps to remember ten golden guidelines:

1. Always feed plenty of forage.

2. Always feed the best-quality forage and choose feed from a reputable manufacturer.

3. Always make sure that the horse has a supply of clean, fresh water.

4. Maintain your horse's weight so that he is in good condition; neither too fat nor too thin.

5. If you give hard feed, offer small meals at regular intervals – don't divide it into large meals. Don't feed more than 2kg (4.4lb) of hard feed in one meal or you will overload the horse's digestive system.

6. Any changes to the diet should be made gradually, mixing a small quantity of the new hay or feed with the old and gradually altering the proportions.

7. Feed according to condition, breed or type, work, age and temperament.

8. Increase exercise before you increase feed, not the other way round.

9. You can feed to complement or make the most of a horse's temperament, but you can't change it. Get advice from a qualified nutritionist.

10. Horses appreciate routine, so try to feed at the same time each day. Good DIY yard owners may ask you to feed at a certain time or prepare and leave feeds so this can be done.

KEY POINTS

- Be aware of your horse's individual needs but remember the golden guidelines of feeding. In particular, remember that good-quality forage should be the basis of every horse's diet and clean, fresh water must always be available.

- Keep up to date, but don't be bamboozled by clever marketing.

- Obesity endangers a horse's health and compromises his ability to perform.

- Supplements can be useful, but must be suitable for the purpose and fed at the correct level. If appropriate, get veterinary advice: don't use a supplement in place of this. Be aware of the rules concerning prohibited substances.

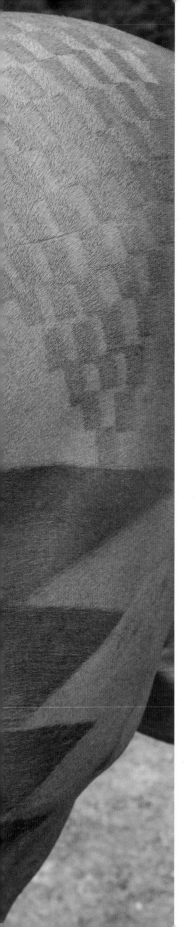

CHAPTER 6

Grooming and Bodywork

If you think back to the time when you were allowed to help look after a pony, or were lucky enough to have one of your own, what activity did you enjoy most? Chances are – especially, at the risk of being sexist, if you were a girl – it was grooming.

Some people believe that grooming is a waste of time and I know some successful riders and trainers who ask their staff to do little more than remove dried mud and sweat stains from horses and give them a quick brush over. Their view is that what you put on the inside is more important than what you do to the outside and that their staff can be better employed than spending half an hour with a body brush. I disagree.

Diet is, of course, important and if a horse receives and is able to utilise essential nutrients, he is more likely to have healthy hooves, skin and coat. But to dismiss grooming is to miss out on the importance of being hands-on with a horse. Daily grooming allows you to assess how your horse feels and to pick up any signs of heat, swelling or minor injuries that may have been missed. It's also a time to check the condition of his feet and shoes.

Also, most horses enjoy being groomed, so without wanting to sound too touchy-feely, grooming your horse gives you a chance to strengthen your bond with him. If you are a professional rider and don't have time to look after all the horses in your charge, make sure that staff appreciate the importance of gauging a horse's reactions and telling you if he seems more listless or irritable than usual, or if he suddenly resents being touched or

◄ Grooming a pony is something all children enjoy.

groomed in a particular area. You will also find that, if you are working with a difficult horse, it's worth making time to groom him, as it helps build your relationship with him.

Every horse on my yard who is in work is groomed thoroughly every day. We also strap them: strapping, which stimulates the muscles, might be an old-fashioned technique but it is just as valuable in helping to build muscle tone as it was in the days when every household with horses had a groom to look after them. Sophisticated massage equipment can be beneficial and saves on time, but I never begrudge time spent on strapping.

Traditionally, horses were 'quartered' before being ridden and groomed thoroughly afterwards. Quartering is a term for removing stains from a stabled horse and brushing him off to make him presentable for work, folding rugs away from the area you are working on and brushing off a quarter at a time. First, rugs are folded back whilst the groom cleans the front nearside and offside, then they are folded forwards whilst the other half of the body is dealt with.

I follow that principle in that horses are brushed off before they are ridden, with special attention being paid to areas where tack rests so there is no risk that any dirt trapped underneath it could cause rubs. Any stable stains are sponged off. Horses are then groomed and strapped, in that order, after they have been worked. Grooming after work is more effective, because the horse's muscles will still be warm and the pores of his skin will be open, which makes it easier to remove grease. You will also spread natural oils along the hair shafts, helping to produce a shine that surpasses any spray-on product.

If a horse or pony lives out, unrugged, he needs the natural grease in his coat to act as a waterproofing agent. However, you still need to remove dried mud and sweat stains and to make sure there is no dirt on areas where tack rests. It's still possible to keep a horse with a 24/7 lifestyle looking presentable – there are tips in Chapter 8 Clipping and Trimming.

THE RIGHT KIT

Ideally, every horse should have his own grooming kit, to avoid the possible spread of skin infections such as ringworm. Keep grooming utensils clean, or you will never have a clean horse. If you only have one or two horses, you have the luxury of being able to provide a grooming kit for each.

On a large yard, this isn't feasible – it would mean that on our yard, we'd sometimes have 30-plus grooming kits to deal with. In this situation, every member of staff should have his or her kit and be responsible for washing it at least once a week, using a suitable disinfectant solution which is proof against ringworm. When possible, we put grooming kit in a washing machine!

If any horse develops a skin condition, then all his equipment – tack, rugs and grooming kit – must be kept separate and an appropriate hygiene routine followed. Ringworm is the biggest nuisance (see Chapter 10) even though it isn't dangerous.

Anyone putting together a basic kit for use on a horse who is stabled some of the time and rugged when necessary should include:

- Hoofpick.

- Grooming kit or rubber curry comb for lifting dirt to the surface of the coat.

- Flick dandy brush for flicking away dirt.

- Body brush for massaging the skin and removing grease.

- Metal curry comb for cleaning body brush.

- Plastic comb or human hairbrush for use on mane.

- Water brush for laying mane (a term used for dampening the mane and encouraging it to lie on the offside).

- Sponges or disposable cotton pads for cleaning the eyes, nose and dock.

- Strapping pad.

- Stable rubber or polishing mitt.

Other items, which won't necessarily have a permanent home in your grooming box but will be needed in appropriate conditions, or when you are tidying a horse's mane or tail or preparing for a competition, are listed below. Their use is explained in later chapters:

– Fly repellent.

– Hoof oil or dressing.

– Trimming scissors.

– Combs cut to different lengths for making quarter marks.

– Equipment for shaping a horse's mane or tail, if appropriate. I use a blade from a pair of thinning scissors; others prefer to use an old clipper blade or a shaping comb/rake designed originally for dog grooming. If you use the traditional pulling technique, you will want to include a pulling comb, but I've found it's safer and kinder to use other methods.

▲ I use a blade from a pair of thinning scissors to shape a horse's mane.

GROOMING TECHNIQUE

Your grooming routine should allow you to check the horse, clean out his feet and check shoes, lift dirt and grease and remove it rather than redistribute it. Everyone develops a preferred routine, but this is mine for the horse who is stabled part of the time and is rugged and clipped as appropriate.

Tie up the horse either in or outside his stable. In theory, it's better to groom outside the stable because you don't spread dust and dirt into his environment. In practice, this isn't safe on a busy yard when several horses may be groomed at the same time and there will be lots of other things going on.

Run your hand down the horse's legs to check for heat and swellings, then pick out his feet. Check that shoes are secure and that there are no risen clenches; clenches are the nail ends that have been knocked over on the outside of the foot. If one comes up, it can cause injury to the opposite limb, so if you find one, tap it over with a hammer.

Next, begin work on the horse from head to toe, starting at the head and working back so you are not spreading dirt over a previously groomed area. I use a rubber grooming mitt to lift dirt rather than a rubber curry comb, because it flexes and allows my hand to follow the contours of the horse. It also makes it easier to judge how much pressure I'm applying. Use it in a circular motion, so you are also massaging the horse, and use it all over. Most horses love this action on their head and jaw and it helps them relax. Using it on other parts, including the legs, improves circulation.

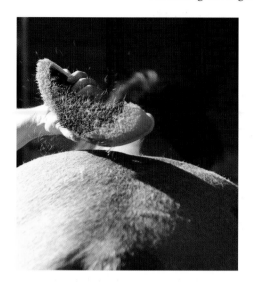

▲ Use a flick dandy brush to flick away dust and grease that has been raised to the surface of the coat.

Take a flick dandy brush and flick away dirt and dust, twisting your wrist so that the brush lifts away after each stroke.

Use a body brush to lift grease from the skin and spread natural oils along the hair shafts. To be effective and to avoid putting unwanted strain on your wrists, elbows and back, you must adopt a correct stance for this part of the grooming process. This might sound fussy, but if you're employing the wrong technique to groom several horses a day, every day, you could end up with repetitive strain injury to your wrists or elbows, or back pain.

Hold the brush in the hand closer to the horse and stand with your feet apart. You should be far enough away from the horse to be able to put your weight behind each brush stroke, thus using your weight to move the bristles through his coat rather than straining your wrist and elbow joints. Stand at an angle to the horse rather than facing him so you don't twist your upper body every time you use the brush, but rather allow your body to roll with the action.

Grease builds up under and at the top of the mane and in whorls of the coat, so pay particular attention to these areas. After every two or three brush strokes, clean your body brush on a metal curry comb. Hold the curry comb in one hand and push the brush over it, away from you. If you pull the brush towards you, you'll spread dirt over yourself.

▼ When using a metal curry comb to clean a body brush, push the brush away from you, as shown.

If your horse has a short, shaped mane that is plaited for competition, it can be combed when necessary, preferably with a plastic comb that is less likely to break the hair than a metal one, or brushed with a body brush. It should also be trained to lie on the offside of the neck so that plaits sit correctly – something to remember when you are pulling or shaping it, as explained later in this chapter. I find the easiest way to do this is to comb the mane through, then wet it.

You may be advised to put a horse's mane in stable plaits to encourage it to lie the correct way. These are made by dividing the mane into sections, plaiting each one and securing it with a band. I prefer not to do this, as too frequent plaiting weakens the hair. Horses who are competed regularly are plaited quite often enough.

Some owners brush tails regularly, using a body brush. Others prefer to use a hairbrush designed for use on people, or a wide-toothed plastic comb. Whatever you choose, start by grooming the bottom part of the tail and gradually work up. This way, you minimise the risk of making or worsening tangles and breaking hair.

I prefer to brush tails as little as possible. This is a rare occasion when I find the answer in a spray bottle: I spay the long hair below the dock every couple of days with a mane and tail de-tangler and run my fingers through it to separate it. As a show producer, I need to create the best picture and, if a horse has a wispy tail, it doesn't match a big hind end. You can get false tails for the show ring – the equivalent of hair extensions – but I'd rather look after the real thing in the first place.

▼ Use a separate pad when cleaning each eye to avoid the risk of spreading infection.

Use a damp cotton pad to clean the outside of the horse's eyes, using a separate pad for each eye to avoid the risk of spreading any dirt or infection. To finish off, wipe your horse over with a damp cloth or a fabric grooming mitt. Some people use car cleaning mitts for this purpose, as the fibres are said to attract dust.

QUARTER MARKS

Competitors often use quarter marks – designs made with a brush, comb or stencil – to show off a horse's hindquarters. They have also become popular with some dressage fans. Don't create quarter marks for the sake of it; if a horse has weak hindquarters, quarter marks will draw attention to the fact.

Marks range from small squares set in an inverted triangle to blocks and sharks' teeth. You need to experiment to find what looks best on your horse, but I find that small squares suit only fine show pony and TB types whilst blocks and sharks' teeth complement most types. If a horse has good conformation but slightly hollow hindquarters, sharks' teeth help to 'fill' them.

Groom the horse thoroughly to remove any traces of grease, then brush over the area you will be working on, using a slightly damp and spotlessly clean body brush. Make the patterns by combing or brushing against the lie of the coat.

I have a selection of cut-down metal combs which I use to make squares of an appropriate size. Some people use plastic templates, but using combs allows you to tailor your technique. For instance, if you start at the top of the quarters with larger squares, then decrease their size as you move down, it helps to give an impression of a good topline.

▶ My selection of cut-down metal combs allows me to make quarter marks of different sizes, to suit each animal's conformation.

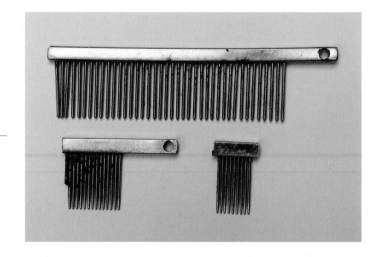

▶ Experiment with the type and size of quarter marks to see what suits your horse best.

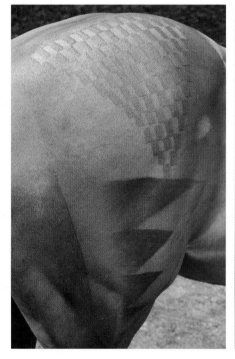

A DELICATE SUBJECT

Every now and then, you will need to clean a stallion or gelding's sheath; vets now advise that this should not be done too frequently and that on average, every four weeks is sufficient. There are many types of cleaning products marketed specifically for this purpose, but standard veterinary advice is that water alone should be sufficient in most cases.

The sheath produces a waxy substance called smegma, which helps to maintain healthy skin and ensure that the penis can be extruded and withdrawn without discomfort. This can build up, especially in geldings, who are naturally less mobile in this area. However, if you are over-zealous, you will remove normal, healthy bacteria, which can lead to infection.

To clean the area safely, wear thin latex gloves, stand next to the horse's elbow and wipe inside the sheath with a sponge soaked in lukewarm water. If your horse resents this and seems uncomfortable, or if there is an unpleasant odour, ask your vet to check him out.

Sometimes, a lump of hardened smegma will block the urethral fossa, which is a small cavity in the tip of the penis. You may be able to remove it but in some cases, it will be necessary for your vet to sedate the horse.

Smearing petroleum jelly inside the sheath can help remove a build-up of smegma if a horse dislikes the area being washed.

▼ Use a leather strapping pad or simply cup your hand when strapping a horse.

STRAPPING

Part of the value of grooming is that it massages the skin and encourages blood flow. Strapping a horse adds an extra benefit, as it helps to build up muscle. Sadly, it's often looked on as an old-fashioned and outdated practice that takes up too much time, but if that's your opinion, please try it – you'll be pleasantly surprised by what a few minutes a day can achieve over two or three months.

Use either a leather strapping pad or simply cup your hand. A pad is kinder on fingernails and easy to use when you're practising the technique, but I find the hands-on method makes it easier to judge the amount of pressure a horse finds acceptable. Work on areas where you want to build muscle – the neck, shoulder and hindquarters – but not on the legs, belly or loins, as the horse will find this uncomfortable.

Your aim is to make muscles contract and relax, so bring the pad or your hand down firmly. The horse will naturally tense the muscles in that area. When the muscles relax, repeat the action and get into a rhythm. Always start gently and build up the impact. The horse's reactions will tell you how much pressure he enjoys.

I always strap after grooming and like to have the horse tied up whilst I'm working. If he throws up his head when you strap his neck, hold his headcollar and reduce the pressure until he settles. When he throws up his head, he uses the muscles underneath his neck, which is precisely what you don't want!

Work evenly on both sides of the horse: I like to count the number of strokes. My system is to make, on each side, 100 strokes on the neck, 50 on the shoulder, 100 on the quarters and 25 on the second thigh.

MASSAGE AND STRETCHES

MASSAGE

Grooming has a massaging effect and strapping will help improve muscle tone, but massage carried out by a qualified practitioner works deep into the muscles and has wide-ranging benefits. Some riders, especially those competing in eventing, dressage and showjumping, schedule massage sessions for their horses just as human athletes factor them into their routines. Make sure that whoever you use has undergone a recognised training programme and be aware that any equine sports massage therapist will need permission from your vet.

There are situations in which massage should not be carried out without medical approval, including:

– If the horse has an injury that has not been seen by your vet.

– If he has a high temperature.

– If he has a skin condition, such as ringworm, which spreads through contact.

– If he has lymphangitis (swelling, especially in the limbs, associated with impairment of the lymphatic system).

The Equine Sports Massage Association points out that muscle accounts for more than 60 per cent of the horse's weight and that small muscle injuries may not become immediately apparent – through the horse's change in attitude, performance or soundness – and, being undetected, may lead on to becoming implicated in more serious injury. Many riders look on massage as having a 'stitch in time' effect: by relieving a minor, barely noticeable muscular problem, it could help prevent a major one developing.

Battery-operated massage equipment is standard equipment on some yards. Some is claimed to have a true therapeutic effect, whilst other devices are unlikely to do other than encourage a horse to relax. That in itself can be worthwhile, but make sure that you know when, where and how to use any equipment.

STRETCHES

Stretching exercises, both in hand and under saddle, can also help keep horses supple and improve their range of movement. There are two kinds of stretching: passive stretches, performed by a handler, and active stretches, where the horse is encouraged to move in a particular way. Ideally, both should be demonstrated by a qualified practitioner.

Active stretches are the safest type for owners to carry out, as the horse determines the range of movement he feels comfortable with. The easiest way to encourage him is to offer a carrot, which is why you'll often hear them called 'carrot stretches'. Carrots don't have any particular magical properties – it's simply that their shape means that if the horse grabs his treat before you're ready, you're less likely to lose a finger.

Always ask your horse to perform stretches after he's been worked, not before. If connective tissue – which supports and binds other tissues in the body – is cold, the horse will be more susceptible to injury.

Always work on both sides of the body. If you ask your horse to perform a stretch that bends his neck to the right, you must also ask him to perform it so he bends to the left. If a horse can bend a little further to one side than the other, it indicates that he is one-sided to some degree. If there is a marked difference, get him checked out by your vet.

Allow a horse to choose his comfort zone and build up the time he holds the stretch gradually. Ask him to hold a stretch for up to 15 seconds before seeing if he can extend it, as holding a stretch allows the muscle fibres to relax.

Stretches must be carried out regularly if they are to be effective. It will probably take several weeks before you see any effect.

Here are three simple stretches you can use with any horse or pony, whether he is a top athlete or a family pony:

1. Holding a carrot close to and at the centre of your horse's lips – so he is less likely to twist his head – move your hand back so you are encouraging him to bring his nose level with his shoulder. Hold this position for up to 15 seconds, then move your hand further back until his nose is level with his elbow.

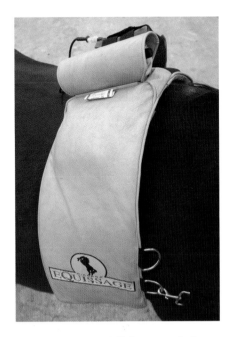

▲ Battery-operated massage equipment is standard equipment on some yards.

This promotes stretch through the mid-neck area which, in time, will make it easier for him to work correctly.

2. If a horse tends to 'shorten' his neck when ridden, which means he is also tightening his muscles, you need to encourage him to stretch forward and slightly down. This second stretch can help achieve this, though obviously rider errors must be corrected.

Hold out a carrot so he reaches forward, keeping the treat at or lower than his sternum (breastbone). Hold for up to 15 seconds. You are not asking him to put his nose between his forelegs – that comes in the next exercise.

3. Position a carrot so that your horse lowers his head, then move your hand so that he brings his head back and between his forelegs. A lot of horses step back to try to get the treat without making the effort, so it's often easier to do this stretch in a stable rather than out in the open. This exercise helps stimulate the abdominal muscles and encourages the horse to lift his back.

BATHING

It's accepted practice to bathe a horse before special occasions, unless he needs to retain the grease in his coat for protection against bad weather. Be considerate, especially in cold weather. If you have only basic facilities, there may be times when washing a horse all over is not acceptable and you should only wash his tail and/or mane.

I always use warm water, not just because I think it must be more comfortable for the horse, but also because it must be more effective. Warm water opens the pores of the skin, but cold water closes them, so warm water must be more effective at lifting grease and debris. I also use warm water to wash down a horse after exercise, even if I'm not using shampoo. Cold water can cause muscles to tighten. (Cooling down a hot horse in very high temperatures, or when conditions combine heat and humidity, is different. We are now told to use cold water to bring down a horse's core temperature, but to wash and walk him alternately rather than leaving him standing during the cooling process.)

If you're lucky enough to have all mod cons – hot and cold water, mixer taps, wash boxes and drying lamps – it's easier to keep a horse comfortable and the rest of us will envy you. Portable horse showers powered by gas cylinders have become hugely popular and are used on many private as well as commercial yards. If your facilities are more basic, it's a case of lining up buckets of hot and cold water and mixing them accordingly, or getting a helper to fetch water as needed.

Always use a shampoo formulated for horses. Washing-up liquid, even the mildest formulations, will leave the hair dull. Some owners use shampoo made for human use, but when you compare prices according to the amount used, even budget ranges will work out more expensive. However, if you run out of the real thing, it's safe to assume that anything you would use on your own hair won't harm your horse's.

Grey and coloured horses are the most difficult to keep clean, and shampoos with brightening agents are popular. Alternatively, add an egg-cupful of purple antiseptic spray to a bottle of horse shampoo, shake the bottle until the two mix and use as normal.

When bathing, as when grooming, start at the head and work back. Be careful when washing the head area as, not surprisingly, horses hate it when a misdirected hosepipe sends a jet of water down an ear. If you're bathing a young or unknown horse for the first time, introduce a hosepipe carefully – some horses will be convinced it is a snake out to get them!

Trickle water from the hose on the ground near the horse's foot, then allow it to fall on to the foot. Work gradually up the leg, then on to the shoulder and neck and along the body. Be quiet but matter of fact. With this, as with clipping and so many other things, allowing an inexperienced horse to watch one who calmly accepts being bathed may help instil confidence.

Some people like to use a sponge to work in shampoo, whilst others prefer a wash mitt, a rubber curry comb or a brush with a sponge set inside an outer ring of bristles. I like to use a brush that has bristles firm enough to reach through the coat to the skin, but not so firm it could make the horse sore. Massaging with hands and fingers is effective, especially when working shampoo into the roots of mane and tail hair. When you've finished, remove excess lather with a sweat scraper, being careful not to press too hard against a sensitive horse or to bang his joints. Rinse as many times as is necessary to remove all traces of shampoo.

HOT TIPS

If you can't bathe a horse but need to lift dirt and grease from his coat, use an old-fashioned technique. Mix an egg-cup of methylated spirits in a bucket of warm water, then dip in and wring out a facecloth or piece of towelling. Working against the lie of the coat, rub the cloth all over the horse, using it from head to tail in a circular motion.

▶ The finished picture – a clean, shiny horse.

The solution is so diluted I've never had a horse show an adverse reaction, but you may prefer to do a patch test before carrying out a full clean-up. This technique is also an effective way of removing grease from a hogged mane.

KEY POINTS

- Grooming is more than cosmetic. It helps promote circulation and also helps establish a bond with a horse.

- Strapping helps to build muscle. It should be carried out after the horse has been groomed.

- Simple stretches can help keep a horse supple. They should be carried out after work, when the horse is warmed up.

- Use warm water to bathe a horse, as this helps keep the skin pores open and makes it easier to remove dirt.

CHAPTER 7

Manes and Tails

Deciding how to maintain a horse's mane and tail is more than just an exercise in playing My Little Pony. There may be practical reasons that govern your choice, or you may need to comply with turnout rules for a particular discipline. For instance, it's regarded as good manners to plait a horse for many areas of competition, whereas polo ponies are hogged to prevent mane hair interfering with the polo mallet, and British Show Horse Association rules require show cobs to be hogged as it is felt this traditional turnout shows off a strong neck and workmanlike head.

◄ Show cobs are hogged to show off their workmanlike conformation.

There may also be times when you need to do some clever thinking, such as when turning out a horse who should have a long mane for one discipline, but be plaited for another. This is when alternative turnout tricks such as running or Spanish plaits come into play.

SHAPING UP

If you want to plait a horse's mane in the conventional way for competition, it should be about 12.5–15cm (5–6in) long and of even thickness. This necessitates regular shortening and, if the horse has a particularly thick mane, you may need to thin it slightly.

The traditional way to shape a mane or tail is to pull it, removing a few hairs at a time by pulling them out at the roots. There is nothing wrong with this if the horse remains calm and comfortable during the process and it is done considerately, though I prefer what I believe is a kinder method, which gives just as good results. However, for those who prefer to pull, keep these safety guidelines in mind:

■ Pull after exercise, because the hairs will come out more easily when the horse is warm.

■ Wear a hard hat and sensible footwear, even on a hot day. The time you choose to go hatless and wear trainers is the time a horse will throw up his head and bang you in the face, or tread on your toes.

■ A horse may become bored or restless. If you have to pull half the mane, then go back to it the following day, so be it. Don't upset your horse because you are determined to get it all done at once: it isn't fair, and he will remember a bad experience.

■ Use a metal pulling comb, which has shorter teeth than a mane comb.

■ Protect your finger joint with sticking plaster to stop you getting cut by horsehair.

■ If you must pull a tail, never stand directly behind the horse, always to one side.

■ If you decide it's safer to pull a tail by backing the horse up to a stable door and reaching over it, the door must be strong and fastened top and bottom.

PULLING TECHNIQUES

Pulling manes

To pull a mane, start by combing it through to ensure there are no tangles and to allow you to decide how much you need to take out. Think about thinning rather than obsessing about a neat edge, as you can create an even line afterwards, if necessary.

Always take hair from underneath as, if you pull out hairs from the top, you end up with a scruffy fringe growing down.

Take hold of a few hairs from underneath and backcomb the top layer away from them. Pull out three or four hairs in one quick movement; if the mane hair is slippery, it's easier if you wrap it round the comb before you pull. Work along the mane rather than concentrating on one section at a time and comb down often to check that you are maintaining an even thickness.

When you have finished thinning a mane – perhaps, as already indicated, over more than one session – you can neaten the edge if necessary. Use either scissors or an old clipper blade. Either of the following techniques can be used to tidy a fine mane that needs shortening but not thinning.

If you use scissors, adopt a comb and cut technique. Cut a few hairs at a time, holding the scissors at an angle and combing down after every cut. This will avoid leaving steps or getting an artificial-looking blunt edge.

If you use a clipper blade, neaten the mane from underneath by pushing the top layer out of the way and pressing the blade against the hairs you need to shorten. Again, work on a few hairs at a time.

▲ Use the comb and cut method to shorten a mane without leaving steps.

Pulling tails

To pull a tail, use a similar technique to pull out a few hairs at a time from each side. It's easier to keep the shape if you work on both sides at the same time rather than finishing one side and starting the other.

In theory, you should be able to take hair just from the sides of the tail. In practice, you may also need to pull from the centre if the horse has a thick tail, as is the case with most cobs.

A BETTER WAY WITH MANES AND TAILS

I've included the information above on pulling manes and tails because some owners and employers may prefer to do this. I used to do it myself, until I worked out other techniques which achieve the same results, but without causing discomfort to the horse or putting the handler at risk.

Manes

I use ordinary trimming scissors with rounded ends to shape a mane – which I know goes against traditional advice. The technique used is the same as described for neatening the ends of a mane with scissors, but you'll need to take more off. Don't cut off more than can be incorporated into a plait and be sure to comb down every time you cut so that the hair falls in a different place. Horses usually settle better if you start near the withers and work your way up the neck and because the process is quicker than pulling, you can usually tidy a mane in one session.

▼ Using trimming scissors with rounded ends to shape a mane allows you to achieve the same results as when using the traditional pulling technique.

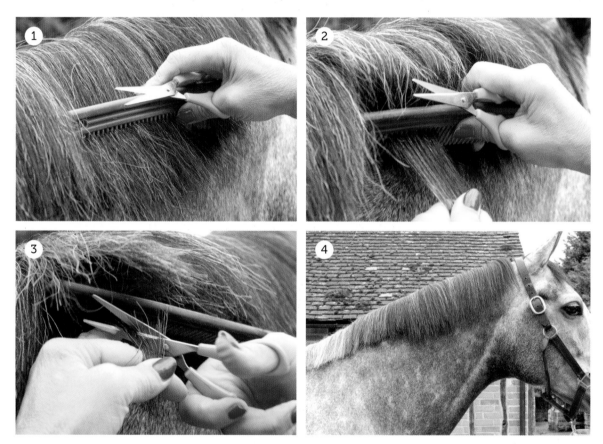

Tails

I use a different method to shape a tail, using a blade from a pair of thinning scissors. If the centre fastening is drilled out, you're left with two separate blades. Each has a handle, making them easier and safer to use.

Use your blade to make quick, short strokes down each side of the tail. Again, with a thick tail, you might have to take some hair from the centre. This

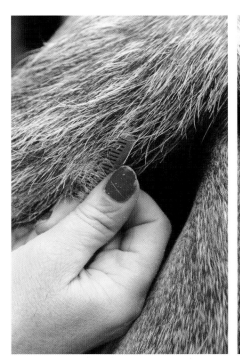 

◀ I use a single blade drilled out from a pair of thinning scissors to shape a tail.

technique will leave an even thickness of short hairs and no one will guess that you haven't pulled it.

Stand back at intervals to see how far down you've worked. I usually shape down to where the buttocks start to angle out to the sides. To keep the tail looking neat, apply a tail bandage (see below) for a short time each day.

Don't use clippers on the top of a tail. It always looks awful! The technique I've just described can quite safely be used on youngsters if you want to show them in hand. Alternatively, you can plait tails, as described later in this chapter.

You can shorten a tail using either scissors or clippers. Unless you want a natural look for a very long tail, you need to cut straight across to achieve what was traditionally known as a 'banged' tail. Ideally, get someone to hold the horse's tail at an angle approximate to his natural tail-carriage. This helps you cut a straight edge and keep the tail at an appropriate length.

Tail length is dictated by discipline rules or fashions, owner preference and breed guidelines. The best length for hunter, hack, cob and riding horse types is usually 5–10cm (2–4in) below the point of the hock when the horse is moving. If you show a native pony, check breed society guidelines. Some dressage enthusiasts prefer their horses' tails to fall midway between the point of the hock and the fetlock, but there are no hard-and-fast rules in this discipline, simply fashions!

▲ Hunter, hack, cob and riding horse types look smartest when a tail finishes 5–10cm (2–4in) below the point of the hock when the horse is moving.

▶ Follow breed society guidelines on turnout if you are showing a native pony.

Tail bandage tips

- Make sure the bandage is rolled correctly, with the tapes or fastening strip to the inside.

- Dampen the tail hair, not the bandage. If you wet the bandage, the material may tighten as it dries.

- Stand to one side and unroll about 20cm (8in) of the bandage. Place the loose section across the top of the tail at an angle and make the first turn under the dock.

- Fold over the loose end and bandage over it. This helps to keep the tail bandage secure.

- Bandage down, overlapping each turn by half the width of the bandage. Keep the tension even. The bandage should be taut, but not pulled tight.

- When you reach the end of the tailbones, make a couple of turns (or more, depending on the size of the horse or pony) back up the tail before fastening the bandage. You won't cause any problems if you fasten the bandage without doing this, but you'll be more likely to make kinks in the tail hair.

- Tie or fasten the bandage on the outside, maintaining the same tension as the bandage. If the bandage fastens with tie tapes and you have been able to make a turn or two back up the tail, you can fold your final wrap over the knot and loose

ends to keep everything secure and tidy. If you haven't made a turn-back, tuck in the loose ends.

- Bend the tail gently into a comfortable position (see below).

- To remove a tail bandage, undo the ties or tapes, wrap both hands round the top of the dock and slide the bandage down and off.

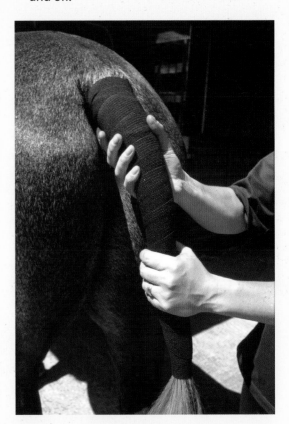

▲ When you have finished applying a tail bandage, bend the tail gently into position to keep the horse comfortable.

HOGGING A MANE

As mentioned, show cobs and polo ponies are hogged, but if you're not sure whether or not you want to take off a horse's mane, remember that it will take about a year to grow back fully. However, if you buy a horse with a hogged mane and want to grow it out, ignore those who tell you that it will never look smart. It will, though you do have to go through the Mohican stage.

A hogged mane only looks right if the horse has a workmanlike head and neck, which is why most cobs can carry it off even if they haven't yet built up sufficient muscle. It doesn't suit finely built horses, though of course polo ponies are hogged to prevent interference from the reins or mallet. Some owners also prefer to hog animals who suffer from sweet itch, as it makes it easier to apply topical products and gives a neater appearance than leaving a half-rubbed mane.

Your horse must accept clippers along his neck and near and between his ears and you'll get a better result if you can get him to stretch and lower his neck. First, run the clippers down the centre of his neck, then clip up each side. Be careful not to cut into the neck hair when hogging a horse with a full coat.

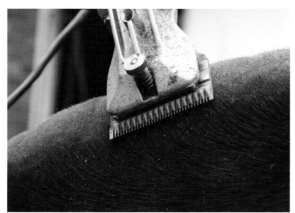

▼ To hog a mane, run the clippers down the centre of the horse's neck, then clip up each side, turning the clippers to give a neat line but being careful not to cut into the neck hair.

If you're taking off a long mane rather than tidying up a horse who is already hogged, cut off the long hair with scissors first. This minimises the risk of your clippers overheating because the air vent is blocked by falling hair.

A greasy hogged mane looks awful, especially when you are looking down on it. Keep it clean by wiping it with a cloth dampened with witch hazel or surgical spirit.

HAIRSTYLES FOR 'HAIRIES'

If you have a horse or pony with a long mane, tail and feathers, such as one of the heavy native breeds or a coloured cob turned out as a 'traditional', you need to mix protection and practicality. De-tangling spray comes into its own and some owners like to put manes and tails into loose plaits to keep them out of the way.

Breeds such as Fells and Dales grow long, thick manes and tails as part of their protection systems: look at their natural environment and you'll see why they need all they can grow. Understandably, owners are proud of their animals' heritage and want to keep natural characteristics. If they show them, 'natural' manes and tails are mandatory.

However, we have to draw a line between what nature intends and what is practical or even humane. A mane that reaches an animal's knees or a tail that is so long he can't avoid standing on it is, to my mind, neither practical nor kind. Nor is 'protecting' a tail by making the horse wear a tail bag – a bag which encases the long tail hairs below the end of the tailbones – for long periods.

The best way to shorten a tail and achieve a natural look is to hold it a short distance above the bottom and keep cutting across at an angle. This will avoid leaving a giveaway straight edge.

Animals with heavy feathers can be prone to leg or heel mites. The mites are usually too small to see, but ask your vet to check for their presence if your horse stamps a lot. They are easy to treat, but a vet may need to take hair samples or skin scrapings. There is anecdotal evidence that pig oil – used to prevent pigs getting skin problems – helps prevent mites and mud fever, but get veterinary advice first as there may be situations in which it can cause problems.

▲ Animals with heavy feathers, manes and tails can be high maintenance.

PERFECT PLAITS

Plaiting a mane is an art, as the number of plaits and the way they are set on to a horse's neck can make the most of his conformation. It can even create an optical illusion, as when setting plaits on top of the neck adds the appearance of extra substance to a neck lacking muscle.

Plaits can be sewn or, if you are practising techniques or in a hurry, fastened with rubber bands or yarn. Stitching looks neater and will keep the plaits more secure. To undo stitched plaits, use a dressmaker's stitch unpicker rather than scissors as there is less risk of cutting into mane hair.

Conventional (hunter) plaits are acceptable for most disciplines, with the proviso that some showing categories – native ponies, pure-bred Arabs and cobs shown as traditionals – specify that manes must be natural. Even then, it's important to check breed and society guidelines, as some allow a degree of thinning and shortening. The rules are taken to extremes for pure-bred Arabians, where the fashion is to cut an exaggeratedly long bridlepath. The

▲ The size and spacing of plaits should suit a horse's conformation, as shown with this heavyweight hunter.

basic technique for plaiting is explained below. Traditionally, there were seven or nine plaits along the neck with one for the forelock. In the UK, it's accepted that you should not need more than eleven; in the USA, riders sometimes opt for many more. Tailor the size and number of plaits to suit your horse's conformation – for some reason, most people still opt for an odd number along the neck. A heavyweight hunter type looks better with relatively substantial plaits (not 'golf balls') spaced apart whilst smaller plaits set slightly closer together complement a finer type of animal.

PLAITING MANES STEP BY STEP

First, get everything ready and in place: it's annoying to reach the end of a plait and realise your threaded needle is out of reach. We like to plait on the morning of a show, even though this may mean working in the dark. You need a brighter light than most stable lights throw, so I wear a cap with a torch attached to the brim. This allows me to focus on the precise area I'm working on. To save time, I thread lots of needles with plaiting thread the night before and keep them stuck in a small sponge so I don't lose them. The sponge, plus some plaiting gel and a clip to hold loose mane hair out of the way as I make each plait, go in the pocket of my plaiting overalls. Once organised, the process is as follows:

■ Apply plaiting gel or, if you prefer, wet the hair and divide into even sections. Experienced plaiters can do this by eye, but it you're unsure, section the mane and secure each section with a band or hair clip.

■ Start plaiting at the poll. If a horse becomes restless during the plaiting process, it's easier to finish off plaits near the withers than those near his ears.

■ Divide the section into three equal, smaller ones and plait all the way down. As you plait, keep the tension taut but even. However, if you want to set each plait into a 'hood' of hair on top of the neck, to give an impression of more substance, don't pull your first two crossovers as taut as the following ones.

■ Turn up the end of the plait and bind it with your knotted cotton to keep loose hairs secure.

- Thread the needle through the base of the plait from front to back, then take the needle through the top of the plait from back to front, so the plait is doubled up.

- Stitch down the centre, following the zigzags made by the hair sections so the stitches are hidden.

- Take the needle from and through the bottom of the plait from front to back. Next, pass it through the top from the back to the front, so you are doubling up the plait again.

- Stitch backwards and forwards three times to keep the plait secure. If you want to set the plait in a hood to give an impression that the neck has more substance, push it into place and hold it there as you stitch.

- Knot the thread underneath the plait and cut it. Stand back and admire your handiwork, but don't be tempted to pull out any stray hairs that have escaped or you'll eventually end up with a ragged fringe along the crest.

- If you find it difficult to make a neat forelock plait because your horse has short hairs on either side, or has a long forelock that you don't want to shorten, make a French plait. Plait down as normal for a few turns, then take in a section of hair from each side every time you cross over.

American button plaits

Grooms in the USA use a technique for making what they call button or rosette dressage plaits in longer manes, using yarn that is woven into the plait and tied. This is nearly as quick as using rubber bands and keeps the mane neater and more secure, though is not as neat as sewn plaits.

Start by isolating a section of mane to plait and place a piece of yarn longer than the mane hair underneath it, at the top. Divide the mane into three and pass the right section over the centre, taking the right-hand side of the yarn piece with it. Repeat with the left section, again taking the yarn with it. Plait down as far as you can, incorporating the yarn with the mane hair each time you cross over.

When you get to the bottom, tie a slip knot in the yarn to secure the plait. Make the plait itself into a knot to give you a button/rosette, pass the yarn through the hair at the top – using a tapestry needle with a large eye or dress-maker's pull-through tool if necessary – and use the yarn to tension the plait. Tie the yarn round the top of the plait; knot and cut off the excess.

If your horse's mane is thick as well as long, you will need to make a greater number of plaits, or you end up with unsightly 'golf balls'.

Running and Spanish plaits

Breeds and types with long manes have too much hair to put into conventional plaits. If convention dictates that you need to plait for some competitions, such as affiliated dressage, you can make a running or Spanish plait. These are also useful if you need to keep a mane out of the way when riding in wet or muddy conditions.

To make a **running plait**, start with a section of hair near the ears as when making an ordinary plait. Plait down, but each time you pass the left-hand section over the centre one, take in a small piece of mane. Let the mane fall naturally rather than pulling it tight and, as you progress, the plait will curve round.

Carry on plaiting, taking in the same amount of hair every time you cross the left-hand section over the centre piece. As you work, you'll create a long plait that forms a neat edge to the bottom of the mane. When you've reached the withers and there's no more hair to take in, plait the tail end and fasten as with an ordinary plait. Double up the loose ends, bind round and secure.

A **Spanish plait** is made using the same technique – but this time you keep the plait tight every time you take in a new section of hair. This means that the finished plait follows the line of the crest rather than curving down and round.

▲ *left* When there is no more hair to take in, plait the end, double up loose ends and secure.

▲ *right* A running plait will form a neat edge along the bottom of the mane.

◀ The same technique is used to make a Spanish plait, but keep the plait tight to follow the line of the crest.

Cosmetic products

There are many products formulated for the competition market to add shine to coats, manes and tails, impart gloss to a horse's muzzle and whiten leg markings. You can even find spray-on colour products to cover up blemishes. However, all should be used with discretion and some may be forbidden under competition rules – so check rule books first.

As mentioned earlier, I like to use de-tangling spray routinely on tails, as it helps prevent hair breakage. It also helps with the removal of dried mud, as the spray provides a slippery coating to the hair and mud slides off. Be careful not to apply any products that make hair slippery in the saddle or girth area.

PLAITING TAILS

If you put your horse's mane in conventional plaits but prefer to leave him with a full tail rather than shaping it, you may want to plait the hair in the dock area. This only works if the hair at the top of the dock is long enough to get the plait started.

- Take a small piece of hair from each side at the top of the tail. Cross them over, then take a third piece from one side. This gives you the three sections of your plait.

- Take in extra hair each time you pass a side piece over the centre one, so you build bars of hairs down each side of the tail, with a central plait. The key points for making a neat tail plait are to take the same amount of hair each time and keep the plaiting taut. If you let it slacken, your side bars will be lopsided and your centre plait will veer off to one side.

- If you pass the side sections over the top of the centre one each time, your central plait will lie flat. If you pass the side sections underneath the centre one, you will create a raised plait.

- Plait down until you reach a level that suits your horse's conformation: usually, about two-thirds of the way down the dock. Carry on plaiting, but don't take in any more side hairs.

- When you get to the end, double up and stitch as before, then pass the needle from front to back. Double up the long plait to the bottom of the side bars and push the needle from back to front. You can either leave the plait as a loop, or stitch down so it lies flat.

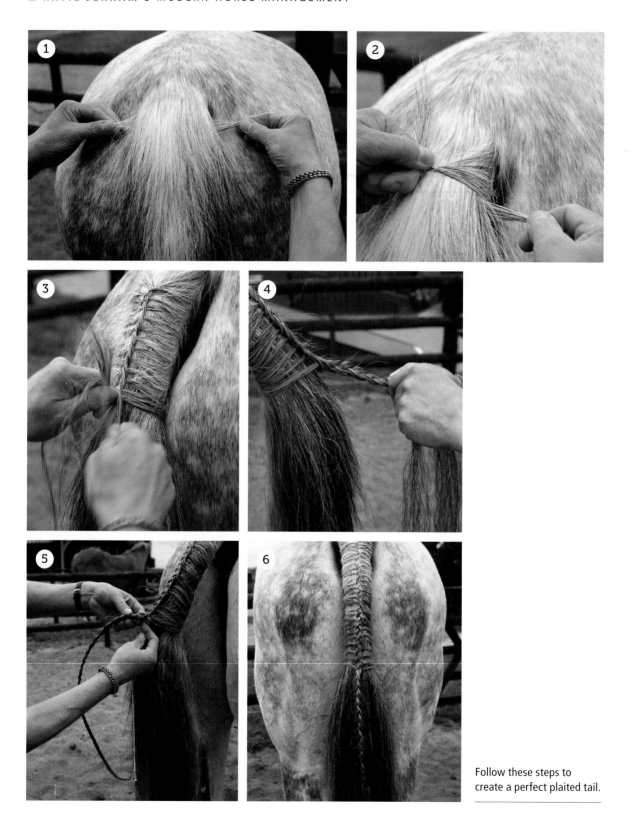

Follow these steps to create a perfect plaited tail.

Having plaited a tail, you can put a tail bandage on your horse to travel him as usual, but you will need to unwrap it to remove it. Don't forget and pull it down from the top, or you'll spoil your work. See the photo sequence opposite.

'Mud tails'

Some people like to make 'mud tails' for hunting, fastening up the hair below the dock so it doesn't get wet and muddy. I've occasionally done this when we've been hunting point-to-pointers to qualify them, but wouldn't do it on a sensitive horse. The tail becomes solid and heavy and, if the horse swishes it, it can hit them on the flanks and provoke a sharp reaction.

There are several ways to make a mud tail. The method I prefer is to plait the top of the tail as described above, then braid the long hairs below the dock into a single plait, stitch the bottom to secure it and finally double up the long plait and stitch it down the centre as with a mane plait.

KEY POINTS

- There are techniques to shape a mane or tail which are kinder and often safer than the conventional pulling technique.

- If you do decide to pull a mane or tail, do it when the horse is warm and only pull out a few hairs at a time.

- If you want to plait a horse's mane in the conventional way for competition, it should be about 12.5–15cm (5–6in) long and of even thickness.

- The number of plaits and the way they are set on the neck can enhance your horse's conformation.

- When applying a tail bandage, dampen the tail hair – not the bandage. A wet bandage will shrink and may become too tight.

- Don't use stiff brushes on tails, or you'll break the hair. Do use a de-tangling spray on tail hair regularly to help prevent tangles.

CHAPTER 8

Clipping and Trimming

Clipping and trimming can be carried out for practical or cosmetic reasons, in that order of priority. It's always satisfying to see a scruffy horse or pony get a smart new look but, in many cases, you can achieve maximum benefits by removing the minimum of hair. Owners who automatically opt for full clips may not be doing the best for their horses and could even be creating extra expense: a fully clipped horse needs extra rugs and, in some cases, extra feed to keep warm.

The underlying reason for clipping is to allow a horse to work comfortably. You don't want him to get too hot and sweaty, but nor do you want him to catch cold. Rugs can compensate in some circumstances, but not all. If you're at a venue with limited warm-up facilities – no pun intended – where time limits are imposed, it can be difficult to keep a horse comfortable and you will need to keep him moving and, when appropriate, use an exercise rug. Muscle groups in the back and hindquarters are particularly vulnerable and if you ask a horse to stretch cold muscles as part of your pre-competition routine, you risk causing injury.

Horses or ponies with Cushing's syndrome, a condition which often results in all-year growth of a long and sometimes curly coat, may also need to be clipped to keep them comfortable. Foals should *never* be clipped.

If a horse or pony is in light work, he should not need more than a minimal clip and, in some cases, he won't need clipping at all. If you want to smarten him up, judicious trimming can work wonders, as explained later in this chapter.

◀ The most important reason for clipping a horse is to allow him to work comfortably.

An unfit horse will sweat more than a fit one so, in some cases, you need to think ahead. If you take off the minimum amount of hair whilst backing a youngster or bringing a horse back into work after a rest, it will be easier to keep him warm. If necessary, you can extend the clip second time round, but remember that whilst you can always take off more hair, you can't put it back!

Don't fall into the trap of giving your horse a full clip because you're frightened of clipping lines. It isn't as difficult as you might think. However, some owners like to give horses who have thick, coarse hair and will be working fairly hard a full clip first time round, then follow with a partial clip. This means you don't get an obvious step between the clipped and unclipped section.

There are no strict rules about when you should clip. At one time, hands would be raised in horror if you clipped a horse after the end of January, but the sensible approach is simply to clip whenever it's necessary.

The same applies to trimming faces, ears and legs. I keep my horses trimmed all year round because it's easier and quicker to do it little and often. The exception may be if a horse is turned away for a long holiday over the winter.

Contrary to popular belief, you won't 'spoil' a horse's emerging summer coat if you clip after a certain time. It's far more difficult to try to delay the growth of a winter coat, something showing producers try to do so that horses look good for the traditional end of season in October. Tactics include keeping horses rugged and leaving lights on longer, though research shows that, as daylight is a factor in coat change, artificial light won't necessarily have an effect. If you feel you have a justifiable reason for trying to delay a horse's coat growth, his welfare must still be paramount.

I don't usually need to clip in the summer months, but do clip before the big end-of-season championship shows in September, if necessary. If horses are hairy, they get hot and it's easier to clip than to have the extra work of washing down and drying off before a performance. Timing is important from a cosmetic point of view and I'll clip about ten days before a show to get just enough re-growth.

TYPES OF CLIP

There are classic types of clip that have stood the test of time but you can adapt them to suit your needs. For instance, a trace or blanket clip can be high or low and you can reduce a blanket clip to leave all the hair on the quarters.

- A **bib clip** takes hair off the underside of the neck and the chest and can make a real difference to the horse or pony who lives out and is in light work. If necessary, it can be extended to take hair off the belly, to just behind where the girth sits. You can go a step further and clip the lower part of the neck and the bottom half of the shoulders – experience will show you what suits your horse. The final clip within this category is sometimes called a **dealer clip**, as dealers use it to make a horse being prepared for sale look smart without having to take hair off his back and quarters. The clipping line extends higher up the neck and cuts across the top of the shoulders down to the belly (or even to the stifle), so it becomes a version of the chaser clip (see below).

- A **trace clip** – named because it was devised for carriage horses and follows the lines of the driving traces – is another good clip for a horse in light work, especially those who sweat in the girth area.

- A **blanket clip** works well for a horse who needs protection over his back and loins. This clip and the next one would often be more appropriate for horses who owners take off all the coat.

- A **chaser clip** is, as the name suggests, popular with racehorse trainers because it keeps a thin-skinned TB's back, loins and hindquarter muscles warm but prevents them sweating up after fast work.

- A **hunter clip**, which some people term a full clip, leaves hair only on the legs and in the saddle area. Originally, this was to protect hunters from the dangers of thorns – though if you're jumping hedges, either out hunting or when competing cross-country – you should always check your horse's legs thoroughly. A small thorn inflicts a puncture wound and these can have horrific consequences. Some owners prefer this clip whatever a horse's workload because it looks smart and makes it easier to groom effectively. It's the clip I use most because it means there are no lines when a horse's coat comes through. I always like to leave hair on the legs and a small saddle patch and am scrupulous about making sure that a horse is wearing appropriate rugs. You must be careful to keep the horse warm and dry.

▪ A true **full clip** takes hair of every region, including on the legs and head. Again, it may be that this approach suits you and your horse and you can give him the appropriate care and regime. For example, cobs often grow thick, coarse leg hair and some owners prefer to clip the legs full out first time round, then leave the re-growth and simply keep the legs trimmed.

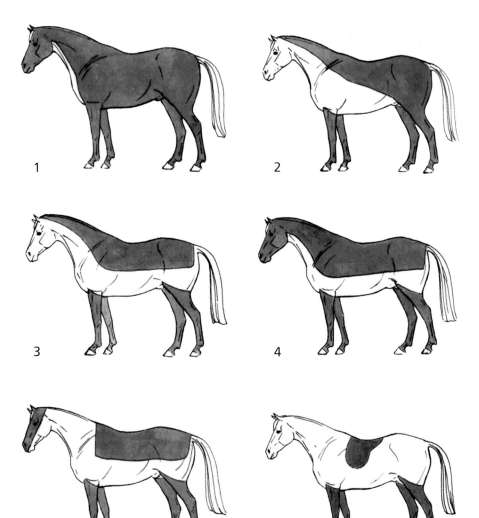

Types of clip:

1. Bib clip
2. Extended Irish or dealer clip
3. Chaser clip
4. Trace clip
5. Blanket clip
6. Hunter clip.

▶ Clips can be adapted to suit your horse's needs; here, hair has been left on the hindquarters to add warmth.

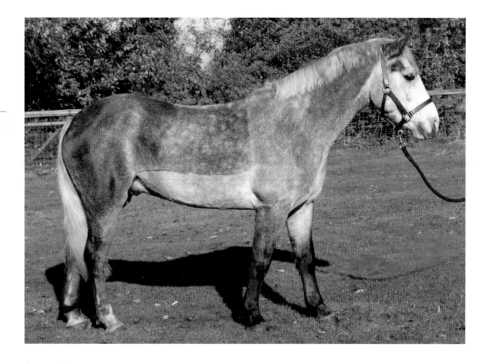

PREPARATION FOR CLIPPING

It's often said that only experienced people should clip, but the obvious flaw with that argument is that you only get experience through practice. However, it's important to learn the basic techniques by clipping a co-operative horse. There are several ways of learning how to clip or improve your technique and this chapter should give you lots of ideas.

A novice owner of a horse known to be good to clip may find that the best way is to pay a professional to do the job and ask if he or she will explain the process. This will take longer, so ask in advance and be prepared to pay for the extra time. If this isn't possible and you have to go it alone, start with a minimal clip and at least ask an experienced friend to be there for moral support. Perhaps start with whatever version of the bib clip will meet your needs, as you can always take off more hair next time.

The more horses you clip, the more efficient you will become. At first, you'll be slow, but if you start with a small clip, your horse shouldn't get bored. You should always allow plenty of time for clipping, but don't add to your horse's waiting time by being overambitious.

Think about safety, whether you're a novice or a dab hand with a set of clippers. The clipping area must be dry and light and the horse must be dry and clean. Applying a light coating of spray-on coat sheen helps the blades cut smoothly through the hair.

Put a tail bandage on the horse to keep tail hair out of the way, unless, of course, you're only clipping his front end. If you're clipping in a stable, remove water buckets or cover automatic waterers. Pile bedding at the back so you can sweep up hair when you've finished.

If you're clipping a horse for the first time that season who has a full coat and you intend to take off a lot of hair, keep a rug ready to fold over clipped areas unless it's warm. Use one which won't act as a magnet for loose hair – fleeces and knitted fabrics have great thermal properties, but if short hairs become caught up, you'll have an itchy horse. A lightweight quilted rug or one with a similarly smooth surface is best. I like to clip in our barn and if I have an inexperienced or nervous horse, I will let him watch one who is relaxed about the whole thing.

I always wear a hard hat when clipping, though as I usually put on my hat first thing and then forget about it unless I come in for a lunch break, it isn't a hardship! If a horse kicks out, particularly if he cow-kicks when you're clipping his belly area, you could be badly injured. You can also get hurt if a horse throws his head up; one of my team got two lovely black eyes after being in the wrong place at the wrong time, for just a few seconds. Unless the horse is quiet and reliable, you need an assistant to hold and distract him when necessary. Even if he's so laid-back he's horizontal, you need someone to lift and stretch his forelegs when clipping round the girth and elbow area.

Don't assume that a horse who is quiet and relaxed to clip on one side will behave in the same way when you work on the other. This applies particularly when trimming ears; for some reason, some horses are fine having one ear trimmed but hate having the one on the opposite side done. You will, of course, check that the clippers haven't become too hot and don't need oiling, as explained below, and that the horse isn't uncomfortable in a particular area.

If you have long hair, tie it back, though this should be a general yard rule. It isn't a case of being 'correct' but of staying safe. You can't see what you're doing and where you're going if you have hair blowing around. Some people prefer to wear overalls when clipping, as horsehair gets everywhere.

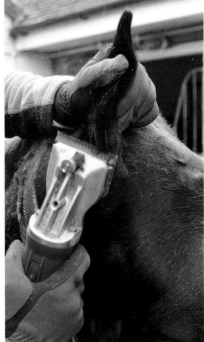

▶ Some horses accept having one ear trimmed but dislike you trimming the other, even when there are no physical problems.

CLIPPER CHOICE

There are so many brands of clippers that you really need to see and hold a set before making your choice. Take into account the following points:

■ Are they fit for your purpose? If you're clipping several horses every season, clippers that are perfectly suitable for a one-horse owner might not be up to the job.

■ Are they appropriate for your set-up? If your yard doesn't have a power supply, you'll need clippers that operate from battery packs; the packs are usually designed to be worn on a belt round the waist. Be careful to differentiate between clippers and trimmers and check that the model you're interested in will cope not just with the number of clips you need to make, but with the thickness and coarseness of the horses' coats. Clippers that work efficiently on a fine TB coat may not be a match for a cob or native pony's natural protection.

■ Are they comfortable to hold and manoeuvre? Heavy-duty clippers may be weighty and if you're a small person struggling to clip a tall horse, they may give you aching arms. Standing on a portable mounting block or similar may give you extra height but this isn't safe if the horse is restless or nervous and likely to knock you off and/or trip over the block.

■ Is your horse sensitive to noise? Acclimatisation to the sound and feel of clippers, as explained later, should give him confidence, but some horses remain unsure about powerful electric clippers. Battery-operated clippers are usually quieter.

■ Are they a recognised make, so you can get them serviced easily? Can you find replacement blades? Some of the cheapest trimming clippers marketed for use on horses' faces and ears were designed for the dog grooming industry and don't have detachable blades, so once the blades become dull, you can't get them sharpened and the clippers become useless.

■ Are the blades suitable for the horse's coat? Medium or fine are usually best. Coarse blades are really designed for use on cattle coats.

■ Will you be trimming a horse's ears and facial area? If so, a good pair of trimming clippers make the job easier. The blades are smaller and the clippers are quieter than those of standard clippers. Some horses won't tolerate the use of standard clippers on their ears.

SET-UP AND MAINTENANCE

Before you make that first cut, make sure you know how to check that your clippers are set up correctly, what to do with them when you've finished and how to keep them in good condition. Clippers and blades are expensive but, even more importantly, your horse will be uncomfortable if you don't keep them running smoothly. A bad experience, perhaps because blades that haven't been adjusted correctly pull at the coat, can make a horse difficult to clip next time – and you can't blame him for objecting.

Read the manufacturer's instructions before use. This sounds obvious, but many people don't bother, just as many drivers don't bother to read their car handbook! You can't assume that instructions for one make of clippers will apply equally to others.

If the blades have to be tightened manually, follow the instructions. Some of the latest 'light duty' clippers have snap-on blade systems which don't have to be tightened each time, but older models and those designed for heavier use will need tensioning by hand.

Lubricate the blades with special clipper oil before switching on the clippers, and stop at regular intervals during the clipping process to re-oil the blades and clean off any loose hair. The manufacturers' instructions will show you how and where to apply the oil. Never use oil formulated for other purposes, or you'll wreck your clippers.

If the blades start to run more slowly, the clippers' running sound changes, or a normally well-behaved horse suddenly fidgets or objects, stop and turn off the clippers immediately. Check to see if any air vents are blocked and clean off any loose hairs with a small, soft-bristled brush. This should be supplied with your clippers but, if you lose it, you need to find a substitute. Check, too, that you aren't holding the clippers so that your hand covers the air vents.

If the blades have heated up, let them cool down, then apply clipper oil. Test the blade temperature on the back of your hand before resuming the clip.

▲ Use special clipper oil to lubricate the blades before you start and at intervals throughout the clipping process.

When you've finished clipping, always clean and check clippers before putting them away. Remove the blades and make sure there are no broken teeth; if there are, the blades won't function properly as a pair. Clean according to the manufacturer's instructions.

You'll usually get between two and five clips before your blades need re-sharpening, depending on the length and condition of the horses' coats and how much hair you take off. If you're only doing a minimal bib clip, you'll get more clips.

Always have a spare pair of blades, so that if one breaks or goes blunt part-way through a clip, you can fit another pair and carry on. They must be sharpened by a specialist, as it's a precision job.

At the end of the season, smear the blades lightly with oil or wrap them in oiled cloth before storing: don't wash them, or they'll rust. Keep them in their original pairs, as they wear to match. Unless the manufacturer instructs otherwise, take off the clipper head, clean off any hairs and remove the grease from the gears using a brush dipped in methylated spirit. When dry, re-grease using the specified product and reassemble. If in doubt, send them to a specialist to be checked and serviced.

BASIC CLIPPING TECHNIQUES

Other than when planning a full clip, you may need to mark out guidelines unless you are very experienced and can clip by eye. The easiest way of marking a coat is to use a dampened stick of chalk. If you need to match one side with the other – for instance, so that the lines of a blanket or trace clip are at an equal height, or so the outline of a blanket clip meets over the withers – use a piece of string to establish your line and chalk just below it.

I always leave a saddle patch, because I like to protect the weight-bearing area of the horse's back. I leave a patch of hair under the area where the saddle seat rests. If you prefer to leave a full saddle patch, draw round a correctly positioned saddle or numnah.

However experienced the horse, run the clippers for a few seconds before you start so he accepts the noise. If I'm clipping a nervous or inexperienced

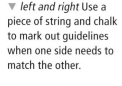

▼ *left and right* Use a piece of string and chalk to mark out guidelines when one side needs to match the other.

horse, I let him see an older, reliable and laid-back animal being clipped first, as this gives him confidence. The unsure horse might start by looking wary or standing at the back of his box, but he should gradually become curious about what's happening and hopefully, will reach the stage where he'll be relaxed.

Start by resting your hand on the horse's shoulder, where he'll usually be less sensitive, and rest the running clippers on top. If he's happy with this, rest the clippers on him in the same place without starting to clip, which will accustom him to the vibration.

Clip against the lie of the coat, with firm, even pressure. If you're taking hair off the shoulder area, then again, this is a good place to start. On large, flat areas you need to hold the blades flat against the coat so that the blade tips are against the skin. Aim to make sweeping strokes rather than dabbing at the horse, and overlap each stroke with the next to minimise the risk of unsightly 'tramlines'. If you've applied coat sheen, this will also help minimise tramlines.

Once the horse has settled, clip along any chalk lines to mark the boundaries of your clip. If you're leaving leg hair as a protection – which doesn't mean you can't trim the hair to smarten the horse and make it easier to help keep legs dry – follow the lines of the muscles at the top. If necessary, chalk out guidelines to make sure it looks right. If you clip the horse's hindquarters, leave an upside-down V at the top of the tail. This, with the extra protection from a tail bandage, means you won't inadvertently clip off tail hair.

To get an even, professional look, stretch the horse's skin with your free hand when necessary – see below. Where you meet irregular hair patterns, such as whorls in the coat and a line down the underside of the neck where hairs growing from different directions meet, you will need to change the direction of your clip.

Don't let your horse get cold. As you clip, he will feel the change in temperature, just as you do when you take off a warm fleece and leave yourself wearing a T-shirt. Keep a folded rug over his back and loins when you've clipped them.

FIDDLY BITS

Some areas are more difficult to clip than others, but the following techniques will help. The trimming tactics can be used to smarten up any horse, though if you're showing, you need to adhere to breed society guidelines.

Don't be afraid to turn the clippers. Horses are made in curves, not straight lines! For instance, hair radiates outwards from the stifle, so if you're doing a blanket clip which removes hair from the lower part of the hindquarters, turn the clippers so that you get a neat curve over the top of the stifle.

When clipping round the girth and elbow area, ask a helper to stretch the foreleg forwards and hold it off the ground. This stretches the skin and eliminates wrinkles, so there is less risk of the clipper blades nicking the horse. You may still need to stretch the skin with your fingers.

If you clip the neck, take the blades as near the base of the mane as you can without clipping into the hairs. Be careful when you reach the base of the ears and, if you need to clip the ears themselves, switch to trimming clippers. I have a pair that I use just for the ears and facial area and I've never had a horse who didn't eventually get used to having his ears done. Do it in stages: close your hand gently round the back of the ear and trim the outside edges. When he accepts this, you can trim just inside, but don't take off all the hair inside the ears, as it acts as protection.

There are two ways of clipping the head: taking off all the hair, including that in the eye area, and clipping up to a straight line drawn from the base of the ears to the corner of the mouth, where the bridle cheekpieces rest. If you clip the eye area, use small, quiet clippers and hold the eyelid down gently.

Trimming the jowl and throat makes a big difference to a horse's head, as it gives him a clean-cut outline. Whether you trim the whiskers on a horse's muzzle is a personal choice or, again, might come down to showing guidelines. Some owners prefer to leave them on because they act as a sensory aid, though I have never had a horse who objected to having them trimmed off or behaved in a different way when it was done. However, don't trim eyelashes.

▼ Whether you trim a horse's whiskers is a personal decision, but I've never known one suffer ill effects.

If you clip off sections of hair at the base of the withers and where the bridle headpiece rests (often called a bridlepath) be cautious. If you take off too much hair, it makes your horse's neck look shorter. The exception may be if you are showing a pure-bred Arab, as the Continental fashion for clipping a bridlepath that runs a third of the way up the neck has become established in the UK.

If a horse has a fine coat, you probably won't need to trim the back of his legs, but if they need a minimal tidying up, run the clippers in the direction of the hair, not against it, and use less pressure than when clipping other areas.

If you want to keep your horse's legs clean-cut, but he has naturally hairy legs – which applies to some cobs – be careful how much hair you take off. If you clip too closely, you can make him look as if he is light of bone (spindly legged) when this is not necessarily the case. I use the little and often approach: run the clippers down the back of the legs, following the lie of the hair rather than clipping against it. Take off as little as you can get away with and trim often.

You're always striving to achieve a natural effect when trimming, so don't be afraid to alter the angle at which you hold the clippers. When trimming awkward areas such as fetlocks and coronets, try holding them the 'wrong way round' and using them with a combing rather than a clipping action.

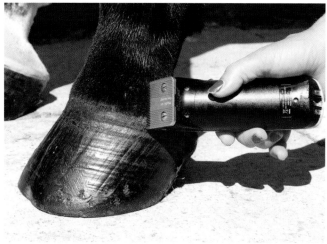

◀ If a horse has a fine coat, run the clippers *with* the direction of the leg hair growth, not against it.

▲ However, it's worth turning the clippers the 'wrong way round' and using them in a combing movement when tidying up awkward areas.

THE DIFFICULT HORSE

Horses who are nervous of being clipped can usually be taught that there is nothing to fear, but this takes patience. Safety must always come first and the handler and assistant must be calm, competent and wearing safety hats and safe footwear. In some cases, you may also feel it politic to wear a body protector in case a horse kicks or knocks you into a wall.

Horses object because they are frightened and there is no point in telling off – or, worse still, hitting – a frightened animal because you will only make things worse and put yourself in danger.

Nor should you make a fuss of or feed a horse who is objecting to clippers until he is allowing you to take a step forward, whether that be standing quietly whilst the clippers are turned on nearby, or holding them against him. If you try to bribe him whilst he is objecting, you are rewarding the very behaviour you don't want. It gives a horse confidence if you are methodical and matter of fact, as in all aspects of handling. Horses are herd animals and you should be the leader.

Letting a nervous horse watch a quiet, amenable horse being clipped definitely helps, but there are also other techniques to consider.

If the horse is frightened of noise, then use the quietest clippers you can find to introduce the idea of being clipped. A battery-operated massage pad or hand-held unit can be an even better starting point to getting him accustomed to some degree of sound and contact. When you reach the stage where you can hold quiet, battery-operated clippers against the horse, walk with him if he moves around, keeping him on a short rope without forcing him to stand stock-still. Take them away when he does stand, so he gets his reward for good behaviour. This may be easier said than done.

If a horse who is used to me working him from the ground accepts his body being clipped but doesn't like clippers on his neck or head area, I sometimes tack him up with a snaffle bridle and roller. I then pass a lunge line through the bit rings and clip it to one of the side rings, on the side I wish to clip. This gives me control over the horse's head-carriage without force, which in turn makes it easier to control the rest of him. My horses are used to accepting direction this way and, because I ask them to stand quietly on the lunge until I'm ready to direct them, or when I want to talk to someone else working a horse in the school at the same time, that translates to other situations.

Some people use a twitch on the horse's lip. There are mixed views on this practice, which, when carried out correctly, is said to release endorphins, opiate-like substances produced by the brain and pituitary gland which have a natural pain-killing and relaxant effect. However, a twitch that is wrongly applied can cause pain which, apart from being unacceptable, increases the risks to your safety. It should not be used for long periods and that in itself may mean it's ineffective.

If it's essential to clip a horse and all other techniques fail, you could ask your vet to sedate him. This is not the all-singing, all-dancing answer: occasionally, some horses appear to be fully sedated but the fear instinct still kicks in. A frightened horse whose reactions are altered by sedative puts you and himself at risk. The other drawbacks to sedation are that unless you are very efficient, the effects may wear off before you finish. You need to be calm but quick and the best approach is to start with the shoulders, head and neck on each side so you at least get time to achieve a clip that matches on both sides! Sedation may also make a horse sweat, which in turn makes clipping impossible.

In most cases, you or a recommended professional will be able to solve clipping problems with one or more of the above strategies. If not, the only other thing you can do is rug up the horse early to try to inhibit the growth of his winter coat. This may mean using a lightweight rug from the end of August, but ensuring that he isn't getting too hot.

AFTERCARE

A clipped horse will be more susceptible to cold. That isn't rocket science, but how often do you see riders standing around at shows? If you're not using an exercise sheet, keep your horse walking rather than standing still and, when he needs to stand, throw a rug over his loins and quarters to keep his muscles warm.

Be prepared for him to feel livelier when he's been clipped. In particular, don't take chances the first time you ride him: make sure he's had the chance to have a buck, either by turning him out with a rug on or, if this isn't possible, by lungeing him. A clipped horse doing slow work may need an exercise sheet.

KEY POINTS

- Clip for practicality and the horse's comfort as well as to achieve a smart appearance.

- Clip when necessary, not by the calendar.

- If you want to avoid clipping a horse, use rugs from late summer onwards, but make sure they will not cause him to overheat.

- Make sure your clippers are up to the job – it's no good trying to clip a hairy horse with a pair of trimming clippers.

- Always follow the manufacturer's instructions on blade tensioning, lubrication and maintenance.

- Always have a spare pair of blades, so if one pair breaks or becomes blunt during the clipping process, you can finish the job.

CHAPTER 9

Rugs, Boots and Bandages

RUGS

Modern rugs allow us to manage horses more easily. Even those with the finest coats can be given protection against extreme weather and biting insects and, of course, rugs can make life easier simply by helping owners keep the wearers clean and dry. At the same time, you need to ask whether rugging is always in the horse's or pony's best interests and must be prepared to keep rugs clean and spend time each day adjusting or changing them.

Rugs become essential when a horse is clipped (the exception being the animal with a thick coat who is given a minimal clip) or if he needs protection from a welfare point of view. There may be times when a horse doesn't actually need a rug for protection, but does need it to enable you to ride him. For example, he won't suffer if he rolls in the mud, but if this curtails your riding, using a rug counts as preventive action.

Use your common sense. Ponies with very thick, double-layer winter coats, such as Exmoors and Shetlands, have a great natural weather-beating system and if they have good forage and shelter and don't need to be clipped, they will often be better off unrugged. Hair stands on end in cold weather, trapping a layer of air next to the skin to keep the pony warm. When it rains, the top, wet layer of hair will lie flat and the undercoat may still do an adequate job provided the pony has adequate shelter.

However, an old pony who is not as mobile as he used to be, or one with a fine coat, will need appropriate rugs. Look at the pony, and at your facilities, then decide what would be in his best interests.

Rugs must be washed regularly, as dirty rugs can cause skin infections. There is also no point in grooming a horse and putting a dirty rug on top. Owners of one or two horses may manage by washing rugs in household washing machines, but large yards need either to install a heavy-duty washing machine designed for commercial use, or use a professional rug-washing service. There are times when my yard looks like an equine laundry.

If you're washing rugs at home, you can reduce the number of times you need to wash bulky rugs by using ones with detachable, lightweight liners, or using a summer sheet or other lightweight rug under a more substantial one.

◀ Rugs must be kept clean, which can mean that a big yard may sometimes look like an equine laundry.

TYPES AND CHOICE

There are so many types of rug available and so many high-tech materials that a horse could easily have a clothing collection larger than his owner's. The main types are:

Turnout rugs, used as outdoor protection in bad weather.

Stable rugs, used to keep a horse warm in the stable. Some owners find it easier to use multi-purpose rugs than traditional non-waterproof stable rugs. This can save time and money – though rugs must still be checked and adjusted twice a day – but the disadvantages are that although a rug with a wet and/or muddy outer layer will dry on the horse, it will spread dirt as it dries.

Summer sheets, traditionally made from cotton and used to keep a horse clean and protect him from flies and light draughts. I sometimes turn out horses in old summer sheets.

Coolers, which have replaced old-fashioned anti-sweat rugs and are used to dry off a wet or sweating horse.

Thermal rugs, made from special lightweight knitted fabrics which keep the horse warm and transfer moisture from his body to the outside of the rug.

Fly rugs, which form a barrier against insects but will not necessarily give sufficient protection to sweet itch sufferers. Fly masks protect the vulnerable eye area, but must fit well.

Sweet itch rugs/stretch body covers, which act as a barrier against the biting midge *Culicoides*.

Exercise rugs, which are used to keep a clipped horse warm when riding slow work or warming up. Designs that fit round the saddle rather than being placed underneath it are easier to manage and more versatile.

Fabric facts

The rug industry has its own jargon. Common terms you'll see when choosing rugs are:

Denier – measures the weight and density of the yarn in a fabric. The higher the denier number, the denser and more hard-wearing the fabric should be.

Ripstop – nothing will stop fabric ripping under strain, but ripstop fabric is made in a way that limits the extent of a tear.

Wicking – describes the way some fabrics transfer moisture from the inside of the rug to the outer surface.

Fluorescent and reflective – applies to high-vis clothing for horses and people. Material that is fluorescent and easily seen won't necessarily be reflective, and vice versa. Both properties keep you safer; it's said that drivers react up to 3 seconds faster when they meet a horse and rider equipped with high-vis gear.

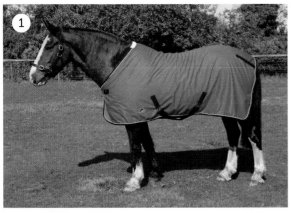

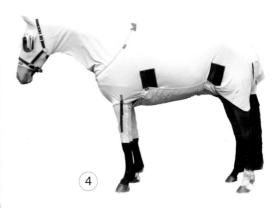

1. Lightweight summer sheets have a variety of uses.

2. Thermal rugs are made from special lightweight knitted fabrics which keep the horse warm and transfer moisture from his body to the outside of the rug.

3. Fly rugs form a barrier against insects but will not necessarily give sufficient protection to sweet itch sufferers.

4. A stretch sweet itch body cover acts as a barrier against the biting midge *Culicoides*.

5. An exercise rug can be useful for keeping a clipped horse warm when riding slow work or when warming up.

Everyone has to work to a budget, but you'll find that cheap rugs – particularly turnout rugs – don't perform as well or last as long as those that have had more thought put into design and are made from better-quality materials. You get what you pay for: as simple examples, rugs with darts at the neck and hindquarter take longer to make and are therefore more expensive than those which are basically a rectangle of fabric with a hole for the neck, and a summer sheet with one chest fastening will probably not fit as well as one with two.

That said, even the most expensive rugs only work if they are used for the purpose for which they are designed and are the right size. A lightweight turnout with little or no filling won't provide enough protection in a midwinter deluge and a rug which is beautifully made and designed but the wrong size for your horse will slip and cause pressure points or rubs no matter how good the construction and basic design.

A word of warning: if you buy a second-hand rug, it should be washed with a suitable disinfectant solution before being used. This is the only way to prevent the risk of passing on a skin infection harboured by the previous user. The risk may be slight, but the hassle caused by introducing ringworm to the yard will cost far more than you've saved by buying second-hand.

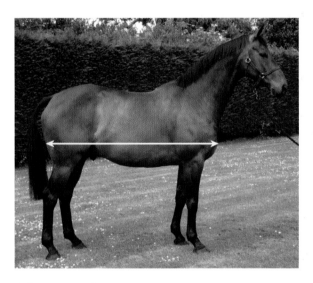

▲ Rugs are usually measured from the centre of the chest to the rear of the quarters.

MEASUREMENT AND FIT

Rugs are usually measured from the centre of the chest to the rear of the quarters and, as most rug manufacturers haven't gone metric, are sized in 3in increments. Ideally, a rug with a standard neck should lie 5–10cm (2–4in) in front of the withers and finish at the top of the tail. Exercise rugs are measured either along the centre back line or sold in small, medium and large sizes.

Don't assume that the taller the horse, the bigger the rug he will need. A 13.2hh pony with a wide chest and deep body may need the same size as a narrower but much taller horse and, of course, the length of the horse's back also affects rug fit.

A rug should be deep enough to cover the horse's body and shaped to allow freedom of movement. A rug that is too small will rub and cause pressure points, but so will one that is too large, as it will slide back. White hairs in the area of the withers are usually a sign that a horse has worn a rug that pulled down and caused pressure.

When it's fastened, a rug with a standard neckline – or the equivalent part of a rug with a built-in neck cover – should rest in front of the withers. The back edge or top of the tail flap should reach the top of the horse's tail.

Rugs are usually designed on the basis that the wearer will have average proportions. As horses, like people, vary in build you may have to shop around for a make that suits your horse best. Again, rugs with more shaping usually prove to be the most versatile. The cut of the neckline is crucial; cheaper rugs with less shaping may gape at the neck, which makes it more likely that they will slip.

The commonest problem is that of the horse with a chest relatively wide for his height and length. If you choose a rug with a well-shaped neck, you may find that you are able to buy a size bigger than the horse needs in terms of length, but that it will stay in place. Alternatively, some manufacturers supply chest expanders, rectangles made from the same fabric and lining as the rug, that clip to the chest fastenings and allow extra leeway at the front of the rug.

Rug accessories

Neck covers add extra cover, but be careful that they aren't too tight or put pressure just in front of the withers. Either problem will cause discomfort and may rub off mane hair. The risk is often less with detachable neck covers.

Stretch hoods, usually with built-in neck covers, are popular and many people use them indoors and out. I use them on stabled horses before a show, but not on a regular basis; I find that they can cause mane loss, though others will disagree. I've also seen cases where hoods which are tight round the eyes have made a horse's eyes sore and other cases where hoods that are too tight round the ears have caused pressure and rubbed hair away, resulting in a re-growth of white hairs. I don't use them when horses are turned out because I'm worried about them slipping over a horse's eyes and causing him to panic.

Individual adjustment

Assuming that a rug is the right size for your horse, it still needs to be put on correctly and adjusted to provide optimum fit and comfort. Rugs are usually secured by T-bars or buckles at the centre of the chest and by cross-surcingles on the body area. You should be able to fit a hand's width between the front of the rug and the horse's chest to allow enough room for him to lower his head to the ground, or the floor of his stable, comfortably. Cross-surcingles should cross in the centre of the horse's belly and be fastened to allow a hand's width between them and the horse's body.

Some designs have leg straps, though these have become less popular. Rear leg straps are usually linked and front leg straps left unlinked, but follow the

▲ *left* You should be able to fit a hand's width between the front of the rug and the horse's chest.

▲ *right* Cross-surcingles should be fastened to allow a hand's width between them and the horse's body.

manufacturer's instructions. Rugs with under-belly harnesses should also be fastened according to the instructions.

A lot of people throw on a rug any old how, but the textbook way is safer because if a horse spooks whilst you're partway through adjusting his rug, it's less likely to slip and frighten him. For this reason, it's also the basis of the best way to introduce a young horse to wearing a rug, as explained below.

Introducing youngsters to rugs

If the horse hasn't been backed and is therefore unaccustomed to something being fastened round his belly, introduce the idea by using an elasticated surcingle. He'll feel this, but because of the give, shouldn't feel too restricted. Ninety-nine horses out of a hundred will accept this without fuss, but if you're dealing with one who is particularly sensitive, you can acclimatise him by slipping an elasticated tail bandage over his withers and round his body. Hold it against him and get your assistant to walk him in a small circle in either direction, then gradually tighten it and repeat the circling.

Get a helper to hold the horse and use an old, clean, lightweight rug that is easily folded, such as a summer sheet. One with elasticated surcingles is best, as these give when the horse breathes. If the horse hasn't been backed and become accustomed to a girth, cross-surcingles can feel restrictive.

Let the horse see you holding the rug, because to him, it's an unusual sight, and also let him sniff it if he wants to. This is why it should be clean, as you don't want to put a rug smelling of one horse on another one. To him, it could be the equivalent of being attacked by a dominant animal.

Fold the rug from back to front and place it quietly over his shoulders so it rests just in front of his withers. Fasten the front, then unfold it so it lies along his back. Keep your movements quiet but confident, because if you behave as if he is an unexploded bomb, he will wonder what's wrong. Your helper will give him confidence, but he should be allowed to turn and sniff the rug. If he gets hold of it, don't tell him off – it's part of his investigation and using an old rug means it isn't such a disaster if it tears.

Fasten the cross-surcingles just tight enough to keep the rug in place. Again, turn him in either direction so he's happy with the unfamiliar feel, then leave him for half an hour with a haynet, keeping an eye on him to make sure he's happy.

Remove the rug as carefully as you put it on. Undo the front first, then the surcingles; this means that if he jumps forward when the surcingles are unfastened, the rug will not be trapped round his neck and shoulders if it starts to slide off. Finally, fold the rug from back to front and slide it off over his shoulder.

Don't forget to unfasten the leg straps and clip them to the outside before removing the rug: obvious, but easily forgotten.

New clothes for older horses

Don't assume that even an experienced horse will accept clothing that feels different from that which he is used to. Leg straps, should you choose to use them, are a prime example. Put the rug on in the stable and start with the leg straps clipped to the outside. Fasten one leg strap and lead the horse in a small circle. When you know he isn't spooked by the unaccustomed feel, repeat with the second strap.

BOOTING UP

Protective boots are standard wear for all horses on many yards, to the extent that their limbs are encased in armour every time they step outside their stable. If you have a valuable horse, then of course you want to do everything possible to protect him, but inappropriate or badly fitting boots can also cause problems.

In general, boots should be used when a horse is unbalanced and likely to knock himself; if he has a faulty action and is likely to strike one limb against the other; for fast work and jumping; if he's shod and is likely to go ballistic when he's turned out or is eager to come in because he knows he will be fed.

Against that, consider that if you put boots on a horse and leave him out all day, you could set up skin problems if he has continually sweaty legs or if mud or grit works its way between the boot and the skin. There are no hard-and-fast rules, as you have to look at your horse, do a risk assessment and devise your strategy accordingly!

Don't leave a horse's legs unprotected because you think it will make him more careful over fences if he knocks poles. It won't, but it will make it more likely that he gets injured. It may also make him reluctant to jump: would you be willing to perform an activity associated with pain?

As with all equipment, boots must be the right size and correctly adjusted. Boots that are too large can interfere with a horse's movement by restricting the area round the knee, hock or fetlock joints. Overreach boots, which cover the top of the hoof and heel and are supposed to protect a horse who strikes into the heel of a forefoot with the toe of a hind one, pose a particular risk. If they are too long, a horse may tread on them. This is a particular risk when working at speed and, for this reason, some riders and trainers believe they should not be used for galloping and/or cross-country work.

In general, boots give protection rather than support. The exception may be designs that are said to prevent hyperextension of the forelegs. These have been developed primarily for the Western reining market, where horses are asked to perform sliding stops and fast spins.

MATERIALS, FASTENING AND FITTING

Traditionally, boots were made from leather, which provides good impact resistance but used to be difficult to care for – wet, muddy leather needs careful looking after if it is not to harden and crack. Modern leather boots can be waterproof and easy to look after and Neoprene or detachable sheepskin linings make maintenance even easier.

Most riders now opt for lightweight, washable, impact-resistant materials and there are some that incorporate an element of stretch, making them a cross between boots and bandages. If you are choosing cross-country boots, an extra factor to consider will be what happens when they get wet: some materials may become waterlogged and heavy.

Fastenings range from simple Velcro or similar touch-and-close materials to straps and buckles. Touch-and-close straps make for ease of use, but don't always stand up to frequent use on synthetic surfaces; in particular, sand tends to work its way in and cause straps to come undone, with obvious dangers.

They also tend to trap hair and pieces of bedding so, if it's safe to do so, put them on and remove them when the horse is outside the stable. The best ways to prolong their stickability are to keep straps closed when they are not in use, or being washed, and to remove debris that gets trapped with special combs available from most saddlers.

Straps and buckles or slide fastenings are more time-consuming to put on and take off, but are more secure. If you use touch-and-close fastenings, designs with double overlaying straps offer greater security.

The general rule is that straps should be fastened so that the ends point towards the hind legs. This is not only because they are less likely to pull undone, but because boots are designed to conform to the shape of the limbs when fastened this way round – so you need to identify which boot goes on which leg.

Boots should be put on so that the leg hair underneath them lies flat, so hold them a little above their eventual site and slide them down. They should be fastened tightly enough to keep them in place, which usually means that you should be able to slip a finger between the top and bottom of the boot and the horse's leg.

When putting on brushing and tendon boots, fasten the centre strap first, then the top one, followed by the bottom strap and any others. This helps make sure that tension is kept even. When removing them, undo the middle strap last to minimise the risk of the boot flapping and falling down the leg if the horse moves, which may make him spook.

Designs which go over the horse's foot and protect the sole – either as a temporary measure when a shoe is lost or as a permanent one, because an owner chooses to keep an animal barefoot but needs to protect thin soles – need very careful fitting. Even when every care is taken, some designs have a tendency to rub the heels. Applying a little petroleum jelly to clean heels may prevent this. The subject of shoeing a horse versus keeping him barefoot is discussed later in this book – see Farriery in Chapter 10.

BOOT TYPES AND FUNCTION

Brushing boots

Brushing boots are the commonest design and are a good all-round option. They should have a reinforced strike pad down the inside of the cannon bone.

Boots made from stretch material incorporating a strike pad have become popular, but are designed to minimise the risk of minor knocks and may not be suitable for all horses or purposes. Some designs are said to offer support, an issue discussed in the next section. Confusingly, stretch boots may also be marketed as schooling, dressage or polo wraps – and wraps is a term also used to describe exercise/work bandages, also discussed in the next section.

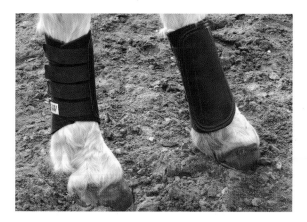

▲ *left* Brushing boots should have a reinforced strike pad down the inside of the cannon bone.

▲ *right* Fetlock boots can be useful if a horse tends to knock only that area.

Fetlock boots

Fetlock boots protect the fetlock area only, as the name suggests. They are sometimes popular with showjumpers who believe that leaving the cannon bone area unprotected means that the horse will be more careful over poles. This is neither true nor fair.

Tendon boots

Tendon boots protect the vulnerable tendon area from strike injury. Many riders assume that they also support the tendons, but vets say that usually, this is not the case.

Overreach boots

Also known as bell boots, overreach boots protect the heel area. Fitting is crucial: they must be long enough to give protection, but not so long that the horse could tread on the rear of a boot with the toe of a hind foot. There have been cases of horses tripping and even falling cross-country when this happens, but you need to look at each horse as an individual and decide whether the risk from an overreach injury outweighs the risk of him tripping himself up.

Petal overreach boots, comprising rubber or strong plastic 'petals' threaded on to a strap which fastens just below the fetlock joint, are designed to overcome this. If a horse treads on a boot, the petals should pull off. Their drawback is that the petals flap as the horse moves, but they have the advantage of being easy to put on.

If a horse overreaches habitually because of lack of balance, work on your schooling and adjust the type of work you ask him to do. Short-coupled animals are more likely to overreach than those who are longer in the body. Ask your farrier's advice, as setting the hind shoes back slightly more than usual may help.

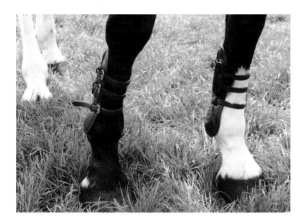 

The horse who overreaches and pulls off shoes in the field can be a nightmare, especially if he has poor-quality feet to start with, as the hoof wall is damaged every time a shoe is pulled off. If the horse pulls a shoe partly off, there is a huge risk that he will injure himself by treading on a nail or on bent metal. Damage does not occur when your farrier removes a shoe, as this entails tapping up the clenches first and easing the shoe off gradually.

left Tendon boots protect this vulnerable area from injury, but do not usually provide support.

right Overreach boots (shown here beneath brushing boots) should not be so long that the horse could stand on them and trip himself up.

Knee boots

Knee boots used to be standard wear for travelling and for exercise on the road, but fewer riders seem to use them now. If you hack on tarmac and/or your horse tends to trip, you may want to use them as a safeguard – though you should also investigate the reason for his tripping.

Knee boots should be fitted with care so they do not interfere with the movement of the joint; the top strap must be fastened tightly enough to prevent the boot slipping down, but with enough leeway to allow you to slip a finger in between it and the leg. The bottom strap is there purely to prevent the boot flipping up, so must be fastened loosely. Strap and buckle designs seem more reliable than those with touch-and-close fastenings. There are also boots designed to combine brushing boots and knee protection, but again, they should not interfere with the movement of the joints.

Hock boots

Usually intended to protect the hocks when travelling these, like knee boots, are also less popular than they used to be. Most people who use travel boots choose designs that cover the leg from the knee or hock to just below the coronet. Hock boots can also be used on stabled horses who, no matter how much bedding they are given, scrape down to the floor. They should not be needed if rubber matting is used under bedding. The same fitting provisos apply as for knee boots.

▲ Travel boots must be substantial enough to give protection but have enough flexibility to allow the horse to bend his joints and walk up and down a ramp.

Travel boots

As mentioned under hock boots, travel boots usually cover the leg from hock or knee to just below the coronet. They must be substantial enough to give protection but have enough flexibility to allow the horse to bend his joints and walk up and down a ramp. Make sure that you fit the correct boot to the correct leg and don't, for instance, fit a boot the wrong way round!

Sausage or ring boots

These fit round the pastern and can be used as a temporary measure if a horse manages to injure his elbow. This can happen occasionally when a horse gets up in the stable and damages his elbow with the heel of a shoe.

Polo boots

These are a specialist design that cover a large area and are not suitable for general use. They are designed to protect the horse's legs from blows from polo mallets as well as other injuries.

BANDAGES AND WRAPS

As the materials used for making boots have become more sophisticated, traditional exercise and stable bandages have fallen out of favour. Ease of application, skill factors and time have also prompted many owners to turn away from using bandages for exercise and work, to add warmth in the stable, or as protection when travelling.

EXERCISE BANDAGES

The traditional reason for applying exercise bandages, which are about 7.5cm (3in) wide and have a degree of stretch, was to provide support for tendons and ligaments as well as a degree of protection. Some manufacturers offer bandages with built-in padding which are marketed as wraps – hence the understandable confusion which sometimes arises over terminology – and American riders also use the term for exercise bandages without padding.

Current thinking is that unless your vet recommends their use, perhaps for a horse who has suffered a tendon or ligament injury, exercise bandages can cause more harm than good. Tendons and ligaments are designed to do a good job and giving 'false' support may reduce their efficiency.

STABLE AND TRAVEL BANDAGES

Stable and travel bandages are wider than exercise bandages and usually made from fleece-type material with minimal stretch. Both must be used over padding. Stable bandages are used to provide warmth and support but, if you simply want to dry off cold, wet legs you may prefer to use stable wraps with touch-and-close fastenings. Travel bandages and the padding underneath them must cover the coronet band to minimise the risk of tread injuries.

APPLYING BANDAGES

Incorrectly applied bandages can cause harm, but anyone who looks after a horse should learn how to bandage correctly in case it becomes a necessity rather than an option. They should be applied with light, even pressure over suitable padding. Exercise bandages/wraps with built-in padding are popular, but the padding may not be sufficient.

The textbook way of applying a bandage over padding is to wrap the padding round the horse's leg, hold it and the end of the bandage in place with one hand and start wrapping down with the other. I use a different method, illustrated in the photo sequence overleaf. By lining up the first section of bandage just below the top edge of the padding, you can apply both bandage and padding at the same time and it's much easier to keep the tension of both equal.

With stable bandages, you should ideally be able to start just below the knee or fetlock, bandage down and make your crossover at the coronet, then bandage back to where you started. If your stable bandages are too short to allow this, start halfway down the leg and bandage back up to just below the knee or hock. Aim to overlap the bottom half of one wrap with the top half of the next until you reach the bottom and make your crossover.

Exercise bandages also start just below the knee or hock, but you make the crossover at the bottom just above the fetlock joint, in the centre, at the front.

With all types of bandages, tie tapes should be tied on the side of the leg, not at the back – where the knot would put unwanted pressure on the tendon area – or at the front, where it would press against the cannon bone. Only one person per horse should apply bandages; it might save time for two people to carry out the job, but each will apply slightly different pressure and you want it to be equal on all four legs.

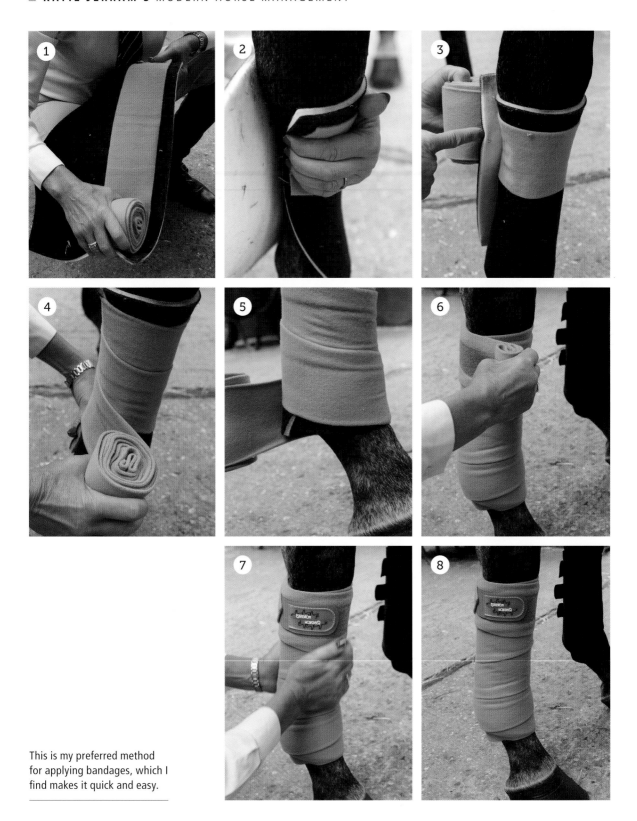

This is my preferred method for applying bandages, which I find makes it quick and easy.

Veterinary bandages should be applied as your vet instructs. If one leg needs bandaging, apply a stable bandage to its partner on the opposite side for support, as a horse will put more weight on the sound leg.

KEY POINTS

- Both rugs and boots must be designed for the appropriate purpose and be the correct size – obvious, but not always the case!

- Most boots provide protection rather than support.

- Don't leave a horse's legs unprotected because you think it will make him more careful over fences. It won't, but it will make him more vulnerable.

- Bandages must be applied over padding and the tension kept even. The same person should bandage all four legs, as this makes it more likely that the tension will be even.

CHAPTER 10

Good Health

As a horse owner or someone working with horses, you'll have to deal with everything from minor injuries and illness to severe conditions. Sadly, there will also be times when you may have to consider whether the best thing to do for a horse is have him to put down (euthanased).

GETTING THE RIGHT SUPPORT

No matter how knowledgeable you are, you will rely on a support network of professionals to help your horse stay sound and healthy and ensure that any problems are dealt with in the best way. If you think of horse care as a pyramid, the owner is at the top, relying on a solid base comprising your vet, farrier and, perhaps, an equine dental technician (if you prefer to use an EDT rather than your vet to carry out dental care). There may also be times when you call on people such as massage therapists and saddle fitters – but in matters of soundness and health, always make your vet your first point of call.

There are many good complementary practitioners, but only a vet is allowed to diagnose, prescribe certain classes of medication and carry out anything defined as an act of surgery. In some circumstances, your vet may recommend some form of physical therapy as part of a rehabilitation regime; for in-stance, treatment from a chartered physiotherapist. However, all practitioners should contact your vet and work under veterinary supervision.

There are times when even non-invasive therapies may cause problems, especially if a practitioner works on a horse without veterinary referral. For instance, an unqualified 'back person' who works on a horse with underlying skeletal or muscular issues could easily make a problem worse. If you want to treat your sound competition horse to a sports massage, fine; if your horse is lame the day after he's worked hard, or when brought in from the field, get him checked out by your vet before asking someone to manipulate him. It's really down to common sense.

It's important that owners can rely on and communicate with the professionals they use. Fortunately, the days when vets (and doctors) were revered and not expected to explain what their patients needed are over. Having said that, there are still owners who are frightened to ask questions when there is something they don't understand. If you don't understand, your vet hasn't explained things in simple enough terms and must clarify anything you're not sure of.

You may want to do more research, but don't blindly accept everything you read on the internet. It can be a wonderful tool, but it can also cause problems. Why should someone who isn't qualified know more than your vet? If a particular herb is of greater proven effectiveness than the medication your vet recommends, why wasn't it your vet's first option? If something sounds too good to be true, it probably is; if you want to try a particular nutritional approach or therapy, ask your vet whether it could cause any harm.

You'll notice that the phrase 'Ask your vet' and similar permutations appear regularly in this chapter. That's because any vet would rather an owner sought advice because a horse *might* have a problem than waited until it became clear that the problem not only existed, but also was escalating.

Your job isn't to decide the extent to which your horse is ill or injured and how he should be treated. That's down to your vet. Your job is to gather information and explain why you're worried. Yes, you might incur a call-out fee for what turns out to be a minor problem – but if you leave it, you may well end up with a bigger problem and a bigger bill.

PREVENTIVE MEASURES

Vaccination, regular attention from a good farrier, dental care and a correct worming/worm count programme are essential for the well-being of any horse, whatever his age and whether or not he is in work.

VACCINATION

The British Equine Veterinary Association says it is important to protect against tetanus, equine influenza and, ideally, equine herpes virus. Tetanus, caused by bacteria invading the system through cuts and puncture wounds, is usually fatal in horses. As humans can also contract it, you as well as your horse should be vaccinated against it.

Equine flu is a contagious viral disease that affects a horse's respiratory system. Apart from being an essential safeguard, vaccination is mandatory under the rules of many organising bodies of competition disciplines. Competitors must be careful to complete courses of vaccinations and renew annual vaccinations within the date limits. Going just one day overdue could see you being turned away from competition venues where passports and vaccination dates are checked – I've seen this happen at some of our most important national shows and it's heart-breaking for someone's work and opportunity to be wasted.

In some circumstances, your vet may recommend other vaccinations, in particular against equine herpes virus (EHV) and equine viral arteritis (EVA).

EHV virus is a viral respiratory disease. It causes loss of performance in ridden animals and abortion in pregnant mares. EVA causes respiratory disease, swollen legs and abortion. Infected, apparently healthy stallions spread the virus at mating and may remain infected for life.

A vaccine against strangles is now available, but it is recommended that it be given to every horse on a yard to develop 'herd immunity'. This may not be possible in yards with a constantly changing horse population, so get veterinary advice on your situation.

Vaccination facts and fallacies

Vaccines stimulate an immune response against a specific infection. They are prepared in a laboratory by extracting specific components from bacteria – the horse is *not* injected with living material that can cause the infection the vaccine is designed to prevent. Most insurance companies insist that horses are vaccinated according to the recommended schedules.

When starting a primary course of vaccinations for equine flu and tetanus, talk to your vet about appropriate intervals between injections. If you are competing under FEI rules or at a competition where FEI rules apply to you or other competitors, you may have to vaccinate more often than if you only have to satisfy the rules of the British Horseracing Authority (BHA) and the organisers of British competition disciplines.

Why should you vaccinate? Apart from the fact that you may need to satisfy competition requirements, it's essential to protect your horse and those with whom he comes into contact. As 92 per cent of unvaccinated horses who contract tetanus die, there is surely no argument against this. We must also remember that equine flu is debilitating, can develop into potentially fatal bronchitis or pneumonia and can have a permanently damaging effect on a horse's respiratory system.

Viruses mutate – it's how they survive. Vaccines are formulated to protect against specific disease strains likely to be prevalent at a particular time. Unfortunately, this means that you can't guarantee that a vaccinated horse will not develop a strain of equine flu – but as vaccination reduces the risk enormously and your vet will only use the latest vaccines, why would you not do your best to protect him?

Occasionally, horses have bad reactions to vaccination. A serious adverse reaction to the vaccine itself is extremely rare; the commonest scenario is when a horse has a local reaction at the vaccination site, resulting in swelling, stiffness and discomfort. In most cases, a few days' rest and bute (Phenylbutazone) given as an anti-inflammatory will see the horse quickly restored to full health.

If an abscess develops at the vaccination site, your vet may need to drain it and/or may advise applying hot compresses. Abscesses seem to cause more of a problem if they develop in the neck area, as they are less able to drain naturally. For this reason, many owners prefer to have their horses injected in the brisket or in the top of the hindquarters.

It's also a sensible precaution either to give a horse a couple of days' rest or keep him on very light work after a vaccination. The National Office of Animal Health (NOAH) advises that vets or owners who believe a horse has suffered a local or overall reaction to a vaccine can report it via the Suspected Adverse Reaction Surveillance Scheme, which is operated by the Veterinary Medicines Directorate.

So what about homeopathic nosodes, which some owners believe should be allowed as an alternative to vaccination? Apart from the fact that these are not recognised by the organising bodies of competition disciplines, there is currently no independent evidence to show that they are effective. NOAH's view is that 'without evidence of effectiveness, homeopathic nosodes may pose far greater risk to horses and their in-contacts by leaving them susceptible to disease'.

FARRIERY

It may be a cliché to repeat the old saying, 'No foot, no horse' – but it's true. If a horse has poor-quality hoof horn, it's often difficult to keep shoes on him. He may also be more prone to bruising, especially if he has flat feet and/or thin soles.

I prefer to keep horses in work shod because I believe this gives them more security, especially when jumping on grass. I'm also happy to use studs. Some people believe all horses should be able to work unshod, but I've seen several accidents happen when animals have been jumped without shoes on and have slipped. I also believe that if a horse doesn't feel secure, he won't go forward confidently and may become more hesitant when jumping.

Overall, the decision on whether to work a horse unshod – or, as a halfway measure, to be shod only in front – should come down to the individual horse, the characteristics of his feet and his workload. Your farrier is the best person to tell you what would suit your horse.

Legally, only a registered farrier can shoe a horse. It is recommended that you always use a registered farrier, including for trims on unshod animals. Some

Emergency shoe removal

Although, as stated, only a farrier can legally shoe a horse, you need to be able to remove a loose shoe to minimise the risk of injury – though if a shoe is slightly loose but still reasonably secure and your farrier can come to the rescue that day, it's usually best to keep the horse stabled and await the farrier's arrival. Once you've started the job, you must finish it!

If a shoe is hanging off, or has twisted, you should remove it to prevent risk of injury. Hopefully, you'll have thought ahead and bought the proper tools: pincers, a buffer and a hammer. If you have a pair of hide chaps, wear them to protect your legs when you grip the horse's foot between them.

The basic technique for removing a shoe is:

- If you're working on a front shoe, pick up your horse's foreleg and brace the foot between your knees. This is when hide chaps offer protection. If you're removing a hind shoe, pick up the leg and set the foot against your inside thigh.

- Place the buffer under the first clench, angling it towards the hoof wall. Tap sharply with a hammer to either lift or cut off the clench. Repeat until every clench is straight.

- Starting at the heel and, working towards the toe, grip the shoe in the pincers and lever it off gradually. Work from side to side.

owners prefer to use 'barefoot trimmers' but I feel that anyone who has been through the full UK farriery training system must be my first choice. Some owners may feel differently.

Your farrier should see your horse every four to six weeks and trim/shoe him according to his needs. It is not just a case of preventing cracks, but of maintaining the correct foot balance to keep him sound. A farrier doesn't just shoe the foot; he deals with the whole limb.

A balanced foot is one that enables the best weight distribution. To achieve it, your farrier will look at the horse's conformation and movement, as well as the shape of his foot, to take into account the angles of his limbs. In some cases of unsoundness, remedial shoeing to give extra support and improve balance may be carried out. Your vet will usually take X-rays and the type of remedial shoeing will be decided on after discussion between your vet and farrier.

It takes an expert eye to tell the difference between feet that need a farrier's attention and bad conformation. One of the commonest problems, which can fall into either or both categories, is the horse with long toes and collapsed heels. This puts pressure on the back of the foot.

STUDS

I like to use studs for fast work, competing and jumping, to give horses extra grip. Ask your farrier's advice about which type to use, as it is important to get the right balance between giving a horse security and preventing his limbs from being jarred. As a general guideline, pointed studs are used on harder ground and square studs when the going is soft. Studs can't, however, compensate for unsafe going.

It's a matter of personal choice whether you use one stud or two in each shoe. I prefer to use two, one each side, as it improves grip and means there is less risk of a limb twisting because one side of the foot has more grip than the other. Against that, there is a risk of the horse brushing an inside stud against the opposite leg. It's a case of choosing between the lesser of two evils!

Put in studs just before they are needed. Don't load or travel a horse with studs in his shoes, as the risk of him injuring himself is too great. Take them out as soon as you've finished your competition and plug the holes; I like to use cotton wool smothered in petroleum jelly or hoof oil. Some riders prefer to use blanks, which are basically studs with flat tops.

▼ I like to use one stud on each side of the shoe to give better balance.

DENTAL CARE

Horses' teeth, unlike ours, grow throughout their lives. Although grazing causes wear, it isn't enough to counteract growth – nature needs a hand. A horse's lower jaw is narrower than his upper one, so when he grazes or chews hard food the outside edges of the upper cheek teeth and the inside edges of the lower ones may be worn in a pattern with sharp edges/hooks. This can cause rubs and lacerations and, because the horse can't then chew properly, he will be susceptible to digestive problems and colic. To prevent these problems, your horse must be checked by an equine vet or a British Equine Veterinary Association-qualified equine dental technician (EDT) so that sharp edges can be rasped smooth and any other necessary measures taken.

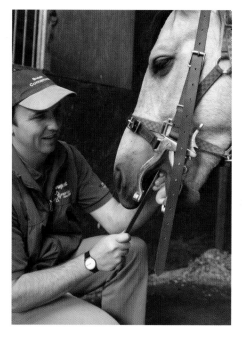

▲ Specialist dental care must be part of every horse's routine.

Many horses have wolf teeth, which are small, vestigial premolars. They can cause problems if they interfere with the bit, but are usually easy to remove. Opinions vary on whether they should be removed as a preventive measure, so discuss this with your vet. Some procedures require a horse to be sedated and only a vet can do this.

The BEVA recommends that routine dental care should be started in a horse's first year, followed by annual or six-monthly check-ups according to the individual's needs. Your vet or EDT will advise you, but if you think your horse has a problem between scheduled visits, get immediate advice: don't wait for your next appointment.

Warning signs of discomfort or pain include tilting the head, resistance to the bit and dropping food out of the mouth (quidding). There may be other reasons than a dental problem, but it is always best to check.

When I'm backing a horse, I always insist that my EDT examines his mouth before I introduce a bit.

WORMING

You can never eliminate parasites, but you need to control the worm burden. We now know that, in most cases, the best way to do this is by a combination of removing droppings from fields, targeted worming and faecal worm egg counts (FWECs). Your vet will carry out FWECs, or you can use a specialist company that offers postal kits.

When you collect dung samples for FWECs, take them from piles that are as fresh as possible and take a small amount from different piles. This will give a wider sample than collecting from a single pile.

The latest research points to the following as good practice:

- Don't overstock fields.

- Remove droppings regularly – preferably daily but at least weekly.

- Rotate grazing with sheep or cattle if possible to interrupt parasites' life cycle.

- All equines should be wormed in late autumn against encysted redworm, as FWECs don't detect these.

- All equines should be tested twice a year for tapeworm – a blood test is available through vets and a test based on a saliva swab was launched in 2015 – or wormed appropriately. Talk to your vet about the appropriate option for your circumstances.

- Always worm according to your horse's weight. The most accurate way to assess weight is by using a weighbridge; equine clinics and larger practices will have them on site and most allow clients to use them without charging. If that's not possible, use a weigh tape and position it according to the manufacturer's instructions.

- Don't overdose or under-dose. Both will increase the likelihood of resistance to wormers; overdosing can result in diarrhoea or colic and under-dosing will be ineffective.

- Don't assume that all classes of wormers treat all types of worms. They don't – get advice from your vet.

Not all wormers are safe or suitable for youngstock. Again, get advice from your vet. Advice is also needed if your horse is kept on a livery yard where owners are responsible for their own animals' worming programmes, or if you run a yard with a constantly changing equine population.

Worming will only be effective if you ensure that your horse takes in the correct amount – if he spits some out, you've under-dosed. Palatable wormers and those in tablet form are easier to administer.

Dispose of empty packaging carefully, as horse wormers can be poisonous to other species.

SIGNS OF GOOD HEALTH

In some situations, such as lameness or severe colic, it's easy to recognise that there is a problem. In others, such as when a horse is 'off-colour', spotting the indications isn't so simple. That's why it's important to know the parameters of good health – because if you suspect there might be a problem, you have a framework in which to assess your horse and can gather information to pass on to your vet.

When you know your horse, you know when he's not his usual self. If an extrovert horse who loves attention and is vociferously happy to see you in the morning suddenly stays at the back of his box and seems uninterested, you don't need to be a vet for warning bells to sound. If you groom him and one limb feels warmer than the other, or he flinches when you run your hands over a particular area, don't ignore it.

TPR

The points above come down to awareness and observation, but there are also distinct parameters that you should be aware of and know how to measure. The vital three are temperature, pulse and respiration: TPR. They should be within these ranges for an adult, healthy horse at rest:

Temperature: 37–38 °C (98.6–100.4 °F).

Pulse: 24–42 beats per minute.

Respiration: 8–16 breaths per minute in a horse, though it may be slightly higher in ponies. Breaths should be smooth and relaxed.

Taking the measure

You need to know not just what is normal, but what is normal for your horse. To do this, you should take his TPR at rest regularly to establish his parameters. In some yards, particularly racing yards, every horse's temperature is taken daily at the same time and recorded on a chart. A rise in temperature is often the first sign that a horse is incubating a virus and should not be travelled.

To take a horse's temperature, grease a digital thermometer with petroleum jelly. Approach your horse from the side and run your hand along his hindquarters – don't just insert the thermometer without warning! *You should always stand in a safe position when handling a horse and, whenever possible, get someone to stand at his head. Children should not try to cope alone.*

Still standing to the side, move his tail over and take the thermometer in your other hand. Insert it gently, holding it at a slight angle so the end touches the rectal wall, which gives the most accurate reading. It also means you are less likely to 'lose' the thermometer. When you hear the indicator signalling that the reading is complete, remove the thermometer gently.

To take a pulse, feel for the facial artery which passes under the jaw and press against it with the flat of your first three fingers. Take a reading for 1 minute or, if this is impossible, count the pulse rate for 15 seconds and multiply by 4.

GENERAL SIGNS OF HEALTH AND WELL-BEING

Other signs to help you build up a picture of what a healthy horse should look like and how relaxed he is are:

▪ If he isn't resting, he should be alert and interested in what's going on. A horse who is relaxed or dozing will still look interested when something attracts his attention, but one who is ill will often remain uninterested and lethargic.

▪ His appetite should be normal. If a horse who normally eats up leaves his feed, try to find out why: don't ignore it.

▪ His coat should be normal for him and for the season. Don't worry if a healthy pony grows a thick winter coat, but if a sleek coat suddenly becomes dull and stands away from the skin when there is no change in the weather, check his other signs.

▪ His eyes should be clear and bright, with no discharge.

▪ Mucous membranes – the gums, and round the eyes – should be salmon pink and, if pressure is applied to the gums and then released, colour should return within a couple of seconds.

▪ He should pass droppings regularly and they should be of reasonable consistency. As a guideline, they should break when they hit the floor, not be liquid or in hard balls – though a flush of grass will often change the consistency.

▪ He should be urinating normally, without straining. Urine should be its normal colour, which can range from pale to brownish yellow. If this changes suddenly, especially if you suspect the presence of blood, call your vet for advice.

▪ He should be in good condition, neither overweight nor underweight, as explained in Chapter 5.

■ He should not be dehydrated. The pinch test, which simply involves pinching and releasing a fold of skin at the base of the neck, is often given as a guideline. The skin should spring back into shape immediately. If it doesn't, your horse is badly dehydrated. This test only picks up an extreme case: even a 2 per cent level of dehydration will affect a horse's performance, which underlines the importance of allowing permanent access to fresh water.

FIRST AID KITS

Every yard should have two first aid kits, one for horses and one for humans. They should be clearly marked and easily distinguishable. If you compete regularly, you may like to keep an extra first aid kit for animals permanently on your horsebox or in your towing vehicle. There must be a first aid kit kept at your yard and all drivers are advised to keep first aid kits for humans on board. You can get advice on what such kits should contain from your GP or from St John Ambulance, www.sja.org.uk. If you run a commercial yard, check whether there are any insurance stipulations.

▶ Every yard should have clearly distinguishable first aid kits for horses and humans.

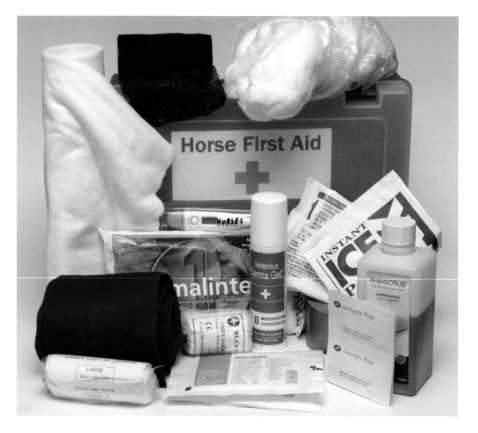

BASIC CONTENTS FOR AN EQUINE KIT

Basic contents for an equine first aid kit are:

- A card on which you have written your vet's contact numbers. These should also be programmed into your mobile phone, along with your own In Case Of Emergency (ICE) numbers – but doubling up means more than one person has access to them.

- Digital thermometer.

- Antiseptic, as recommended by your vet. Antiseptic wipes are especially useful for a travelling first aid kit.

- Water-soluble wound gel, as recommended by your vet.

- Large roll of cotton wool.

- Scissors with curved ends.

- Gamgee or similar.

- Poultice.

- Duct tape for securing poultice.

- Dressings – non-stick dressings to cover wounds; self-adhesive bandages; cool bandages or packs with a cooling action to apply to limbs; cotton stretch bandages.

WHEN PROBLEMS ARISE

INITIAL MEASURES

If you have to deal with a horse who is injured or ill, one of the best things you can do for him is to stay calm. At the risk of repeating myself, call your vet if you don't know whether a situation is serious, or are not sure how to deal with it. For example, a puncture wound caused by penetration of a sharp object may look insignificant, but can be deep. If left, deep-seated infection may develop. Early diagnosis and treatment will assist your horse's recovery, so if in doubt, call!

The more information your vet has, the easier it is to give advice over the phone. This is where mobile phones can be useful – for instance, you can take a picture of a wound and send this to your vet. This may help the vet decide whether you can carry out initial first aid pending veterinary reassessment the next day, or whether you need to take the horse to a veterinary clinic for immediate attention, or whether to arrange a home visit.

If your horse seems off-colour, or you think he may have colic, it will help your vet's over-the-phone assessment if you can take the animal's temperature before calling. Only attempt this if you can do it safely.

The following section looks at some of the conditions a horse owner may have to deal with. It can only be an overview and inevitably, is a chapter of doom and disaster. However, it's better to be aware of what could happen than to be caught out because you didn't spot a possible problem.

IT'S AN EMERGENCY!

Some situations should always be looked on as actual or potential emergencies, no matter how capable the horse's owner. Don't think twice: dial that number.

Colic

This describes any sort of abdominal pain and can range from mild discomfort to a life-threatening episode requiring surgery. Signs may include any or several of the following:

■ Raised temperature.

■ Sweating.

■ Stamping and shifting weight.

■ Looking at, biting or cow-kicking the flanks.

■ Rolling whilst showing signs of discomfort.

■ Standing as if trying to urinate.

■ Failing to pass droppings.

Strategy – take the horse's temperature if it's safe to do so. Don't struggle to take the temperature of a distressed horse who is difficult to handle: never put yourself at risk. Call your vet and act on instructions until he or she arrives.

Severe wounds

These are defined as:

■ Any that is causing severe lameness.

■ A wound that is more than 5cm (2in) long and has gone through the skin.

- Presence or suspected presence of a foreign body, perhaps a piece of wood or a nail.

- A wound in or near a joint.

- Heavy bleeding.

- Bleeding in spurts, which is a sign of arterial blood loss.

- Any wound in a horse who is not protected against tetanus.

Strategy – if blood is spurting and you know how to apply a pressure bandage, do so. If not, apply pressure with a clean pad, if one is available, until your vet arrives.

If a nail or other foreign body causes a penetration wound, it's best to leave it until you've spoken to your vet; sometimes, trying to remove it can cause more problems. The exception is when a nail or other foreign object penetrates the foot and the horse is weight-bearing, because it may be pushed further in. When you've removed it, mark the entrance point by drawing a circle round it with felt-tipped pen if possible.

Bleeding from the nose not associated with fast exercise may mean that the horse has suffered a blow on the head, such as a kick from a field mate. There is a risk of skull fracture: call your vet immediately.

Copious bleeding after fast work is usually a sign of exercise-induced pulmonary haemorrhage. Again, you need veterinary advice.

Suspected fracture/severe lameness

If a horse can't bear weight on one limb or suddenly goes badly lame, try to keep him still. Unless the limb appears deformed or is held at a strange angle, check that there are no stones or other foreign bodies lodged in the foot.

Lameness usually shows only in trot, so any lameness in walk should be treated as severe and dealt with as above. Try to keep calm, as severe lameness can be caused by things other than severe injury, such as abscesses.

Strategy – if there is no simple cause and solution, such as a stone which can be removed, call your vet. If you're away from the yard, perhaps because you're out hacking or you've gone to bring in your horse from the field and have found that he's badly lame, don't try to walk him until your vet gets there. If you are on a public road – where, hopefully, you will be wearing high-vis clothing – keep to the side of the road. Call the police so they know where you are and can, if necessary, send someone to help keep you and other road users safe until the vet arrives.

Collapse or unable to get up

Strategy – call your vet immediately. If your horse collapses on a road, also call the police, as above.

Choke

This is the equine version of food 'going down the wrong way'. Signs include stopping eating part of the way through a feed, stretching the neck and looking uncomfortable, and food and saliva appearing from the nostrils.

Strategy – if the horse is stabled, remove any food and call your vet. Most cases clear themselves fairly quickly, but don't take chances. Your vet may suggest you watch the horse for a short time and call back if things don't improve – unless, of course, the horse is in distress – but making the call will alert your vet.

Laminitis

This condition is very painful and must be treated by your vet at the first suspicion. In simple terms, it is evidenced by inflammation of the laminae (leaf-like structures inside the foot). It is often linked to obesity, but it can be linked to other causes, including concussion, Cushing's syndrome and problems associated with foaling. In theory, a horse can develop laminitis in any foot or feet, but in practice, it is usually seen in the forefeet.

Signs range from slight lameness – which, if it affects both forefeet, may manifest as a shortening of the stride, reluctance to go forward or both – and a raised digital pulse to, in severe cases, the horse refusing to move and taking a backward-leaning stance to relieve pressure on his feet. How to take a digital pulse is shown in the section on lameness (see page 147). Treatment for laminitis includes medication and, in some cases, remedial farriery.

Strategy – call your vet immediately.

Preventive action – monitor your horse's weight and maintain an appropriate exercise regime. Many vets believe that a horse who has suffered a bout of laminitis will always be susceptible to it. In some cases, remedial farriery will form part of the treatment.

Grass sickness

This is a potentially fatal condition and the most popular theory amongst researchers is that it is caused by a soil-borne bacterium called *Clostridium botulinum*. It produces symptoms similar to colic and, in acute cases, the horse will lose weight drastically and quickly.

Strategy – call your vet immediately so that the correct diagnosis can be made.

Preventive action – grass sickness can affect any equine, but most commonly strikes those aged between 5 and 9 years. In the UK the danger period for its occurrence is roughly May to July, though it is also seen at other times. Your vet may advise moving animals kept where grass sickness cases have occurred to different premises during high-risk times, if possible. You may also be advised to feed hay or haylage as well as allowing the horse to graze.

Strangles

This infectious disease can prove fatal. Signs include a high temperature, nasal discharge and abscesses in the head and neck area. Always call your vet if you suspect strangles. On the advice of my vets, I no longer allow a horse on my yard unless he has been swabbed to show that he is not a carrier.

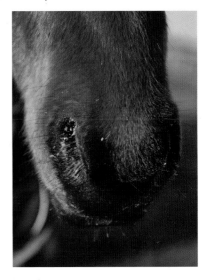

A vaccine against strangles is now available (see Vaccination page 132). It, and regular boosters, should be given to all the horses on the yard, so talk to your vet about your situation.

If strangles may or does affect a yard, the owners should voluntarily go on shut-down, limiting contact with horses from outside and imposing a strict hygiene protocol. Your vet will advise you on best practice, but it includes:

▧ Suspected cases should be isolated until the risk is ruled out or confirmed. Take horses' temperatures twice daily, as a raised temperature is a warning sign.

▲ Nasal discharge could be a warning sign of strangles.

▧ Keep a disinfectant foot bath outside isolation stables and at the yard entrance.

▧ Be open and honest. The presence of strangles is not a sign of bad management – it is bad luck. However, you must tell everyone who visits the yard, including farriers and those who make deliveries, so that they can make your yard their last call of the day and take hygiene precautions. Warn nearby horse owners and riders to keep their distance.

▧ Owners of seemingly healthy horses on the yard must be responsible and ensure that their horses do not have contact with others. This will curtail competition and, perhaps, hacking out, but is essential.

▧ Try to ensure that those looking after suspected or actual cases do not have contact with other horses. If this is impossible, they must follow your vet's instructions on washing hands and changing and washing clothes.

OTHER COMMON PROBLEMS

This section gives you information about various problems you may have to deal with. Once again: if in doubt, call your vet. There may be times when a vet thinks a visit may be necessary and it turns out to be a minor problem. You can't expect a vet to be psychic and, in any case, you should never begrudge a call-out fee. It is far better to be safe than sorry.

Cushing's disease

This disorder of the endocrine system commonly affects animals over 15 years old and is more common in ponies than in horses. Signs may include puzzling bouts of laminitis that can't be linked to the usual causes; lethargy; increased drinking and urination. The horse's coat often becomes longer and may also become curly.

Your vet will test for the disease and may suggest medication. Management is important and you may need to clip all year round to keep the horse comfortable. Since Cushing's affects the immune system, it's important to do all you can to support this. Again, your vet will help.

Head-shaking

We now know that in most – if not all – cases, head-shaking is related to discomfort or pain in the trigeminal nerve, which is the main sensory nerve to the face.

▼ Nose nets are now permitted in most disciplines, but are still regarded as unacceptable in the show ring.

It can be triggered by stimuli ranging from bright sunlight to insects and research shows that about a third of those horses affected suffer only during the spring and summer months. This means that if you buy a horse during the winter and do not know his history, you have to accept that there is a risk he will develop the condition. To put this risk into perspective, it is thought that head-shaking affects 1–2 per cent of horses in the UK.

True head-shaking is usually characterised by a very quick flick of the head. A head-shaker is not the same as the horse who tosses his head in the air, either because he is trying to evade the rider's hands or is tired. It must be diagnosed by your vet, who will rule out obvious causes such as dental pain and ear mites.

The use of a nose net improves or even removes signs of discomfort in some cases. It is thought that the constant touch of the net against the nose deactivates the sensitisation. If a nose net is not successful, surgical intervention may succeed in some cases. Although nose nets are now permitted in most disciplines, they are still frowned upon in the show ring because they point to a condition that affects the horse's rideability.

Lameness

This is the most common reason for horses being off work. Whilst it isn't always an emergency and some cases may resolve quickly when a horse is rested, it's always best to ask your vet's advice. This enables a vet to put together a picture of what might be happening.

If you aren't sure which is the affected leg, watch the horse being trotted away and then back to you on a loose lead rope. A horse who is lame in a foreleg will lift his head as the lame leg meets the ground and lower it as the sound leg hits the ground. An easy way to remember this is that his head 'sinks on the sound leg'.

It's more difficult to spot when a horse is lame in both forelegs, but his stride will be shorter than usual and he will be reluctant to go forward.

Hind leg lameness is the most difficult to identify and you need to see the horse trotted away from you. He will raise the hip on the lame side more obviously, to try to avoid taking much weight on that leg.

By far the most common site of lameness is in the foot, perhaps indicative of an abscess, puncture wound or laminitis. In the case of laminitis, there is likely to be a stronger than normal digital pulse. You should feel for a digital pulse as shown.

A vet may use flexion tests, in which a limb is held and flexed for a short time before the horse is trotted away, to help identify the site of the lameness. Research has shown that hind limb lameness is associated with many cases of saddle slippage, so if you are having saddle-fitting problems, this may be something to take into account. There are, of course, lots of other potential causes, including a rider who habitually puts more weight on one stirrup than the other.

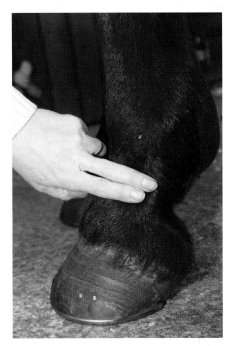

▲ How to feel the digital pulse.

Rain scald and mud fever

Both these skin conditions are caused by a bacterium called *Dermatophilus congolensis* and show as a sticky secretion causing tufts of hair and/or scabs. Your vet may want to take a skin sample to confirm a diagnosis.

There are conflicting views on management and treatment, as some people believe that if the horse has natural leg feather, it should be left as a protective barrier. The other school of thought is that leg feather worsens the risk and the problem. Most vets advise that the best treatment is to clip affected areas, wash with anti-bacterial scrub to remove scabs and keep the area dry. In severe cases, antibiotics may be needed.

Leg wraps that wick away moisture and help the area dry more quickly can be useful in managing mud fever. If the horse or pony in question is of a breed or type required to keep full leg feather for the show ring, you need to think seriously about how you manage him and ensure that his welfare comes first.

▲ Ringworm is a highly infectious fungal condition and although it is not dangerous, it can be a real nuisance.

Ringworm

Although it isn't serious in itself, ringworm is a nuisance. Contrary to the name, no parasites are involved: it is a highly infectious fungal condition that can be spread between species. If your horse gets ringworm, you could, too!

As mentioned in Chapter 2, there is an incubation period of between four and fourteen days (sometimes longer) for ringworm and the first visible signs that a horse has the condition are usually raised tufts of hair, often in areas where tack touches. When the hair falls out, the skin underneath is scaly or bald. Your vet will probably want to take a sample to confirm a diagnosis, and treatment ranges from medicated washes to medication.

Everything that the horse has been in contact with must be cleaned with a solution that kills ringworm. This includes tack, rugs and grooming brushes and stable structures. In theory, even field fencing should be treated, but for obvious reasons, this isn't practical.

Ensuring that every horse has his own tack, grooming kit and clothing helps prevent the spread of ringworm.

Sarcoids

These unsightly growths must never be ignored. Always get your vet to look at a suspected sarcoid, as there are different options for treatment. Never try to treat them yourself, or you may make the situation worse.

Sweet itch

This common condition is an allergic reaction to the biting midge *Culicoides*, which is active during mild weather. It causes itching and, in severe cases, a sufferer will rub until affected areas – usually the mane and tail – are raw and bleeding. Preventive measures may be enough to control mild cases, but if you can't keep your horse comfortable this way, talk to your vet. Medication can be prescribed and researchers are getting close to finding a vaccination against sweet itch.

Preventive measures include:

- If your horse is stabled part of the time, keep him in at dawn and dusk, when the midges are most active.

- If possible, avoid grazing near water, as midges love it. If this is impossible, follow other guidance scrupulously.

- Use a long-lasting fly repellent and ask your vet for recommendations.

- Use a stretch body cover and, if necessary, a hood designed from special fabric which midges can't bite through. Ordinary fly rugs are not enough.

Wounds

Response to serious wounds was discussed earlier in this chapter. For non-emergency wounds, follow the four Cs: Clot, Check, Clean and Cover.

1. Stop immediate bleeding. Check the wound's position and size and try to assess whether it might need stitching or stapling.

2. Wash gently, allowing water to fall from above the wound to clean out dirt which may cause infection. *Don't* use water at high pressure, as this may send dirt deeper into the wound.

3. If you are calling your vet, apply a clean pad and bandage to keep the area clean unless you are applying pressure to restrict arterial bleeding. Don't apply powders or creams, as your vet will have to clean them off to inspect the wound.

4. Wounds that do not need closing often heal best if a water-soluble wound gel is applied. These are marketed under various names.

THE END OF THE ROAD

At some time in your horse-owning life, you may have to make the last decision you can for your horse. Euthanasia is never easy to come to terms with, whether it is a decision forced by injury or untreatable illness, or one you have to make because your horse no longer has a reasonable quality of life. If you are at or near home, your own vet will help you to make the right decision and guide you through all that needs to be done. If you are away from home – perhaps at a competition – and have to rely on an emergency vet, remember that he or she will have the experience and knowledge to help you do the best for your horse.

Deciding whether to have a horse put down because he can no longer work, even if he is sound when turned out in the field, is an incredibly difficult decision. It is even worse if finances and circumstances mean that you have to choose between keeping a horse in retirement, perhaps for many years, and being able to own one that you can ride. Only you can make that choice and keeping a horse in retirement and, at the same time, resenting the fact that you can't ride him, is not recommended.

On the other hand, if you feel it's wrong to euthanase a horse who could have a comfortable retirement and are prepared to give him the same care and attention as when he was in work, that is also your choice. The essential point is that he must still have good quality of life.

KEY POINTS

- Establish a good relationship with your vet, farrier and other qualified practitioners.

- Make sure your horse is vaccinated against tetanus, equine flu and anything else your vet feels is appropriate for your situation.

- Ensure that good regimes are in place for farriery, dental care and worming.

- Recognise signs of good health.

- Know how to take your horse's temperature and measure pulse and respiration rates.

- Put together first aid kits for horses and humans.

CHAPTER 11

Transport and Care away from Home

HORSE TRANSPORT AND THE LAW

You must understand the legislation covering horse transport, whether you drive a horsebox or tow a trailer. For example, if you drive a horsebox over 3.5 tonnes as part of your living, which includes working as a groom or a professional rider, you now need to hold a certificate of professional competence. Those who passed the relevant driving test before September 2009 have 'acquired' or 'grandfather' rights but should still have completed the periodic training element of the qualification before September 2014. If they haven't done so, they have forfeited acquired rights.

In addition to the issue of classes of horsebox and who is permitted to drive them there is legislation concerning weight restrictions, the difference between private and commercial use and whether a driver of a towing vehicle is required to pass a trailer towing test. (*If you tow a trailer, make sure your vehicle is capable of it.*)

It is a complicated subject, but must be understood to avoid breaking the law and potentially incurring heavy penalties. Government websites such as the ones below are a good place to find information:

– Driver and Vehicle Licensing Agency www.dvla.gov.uk

– Vehicle and Operator Services Agency www.vosa.gov.uk

– Department of Environment, Food and Rural Affairs www.defra.gov.uk

Passports

The law states that whenever you travel your horse, however short the journey, you must have his passport with you. Officials from government agencies sometimes carry out spot inspections at large shows and if you don't have the necessary documentation, you could be liable to a fine.

STAYING SAFE

A main reason for the laws relating to horseboxes, trailers and towing vehicles is the safety of occupants and other road users. However, in addition to basic compliance with legal requirements, you can enhance your safety and that of your horses by ensuring that your vehicle is properly maintained.

Maintaining horseboxes, towing vehicles and trailers is beyond the scope of this book. However, because it's such a safety issue, make sure you know what you can and must do and when you need to call on an expert.

Major horsebox maintenance is a job for a professional, though you still need to keep your vehicle clean and tidy and, when appropriate, disinfect it. (Both horseboxes and trailers should be mucked out as soon as you get home from a show.) Although it may sound obvious, keep your horsebox battery charged so that you don't suddenly discover that your box won't start.

Compared to a horsebox, a trailer is mechanically simple. However, it still needs to be checked before every trip and maintained and serviced regularly.

Read your trailer manual. This will give you vital information such as correct tyre pressures, which are often much higher than those for the average car and must be checked before every trip.

▼ The tyres on both your car and trailer, including spares, must have a good tread.

The tyres on both your car and trailer, including spares, must have a good tread. The legal minimum is 1.6mm over the central 75 per cent of their width for the whole circumference, but this offers little grip on wet roads and anything under 3mm may be inadequate.

The tyre walls must be in good condition, with no deep cuts or bulges. Punctures can still happen, so it's a good idea to carry a special wedge-shaped trailer lift. This sort of design is safer than a conventional jack, because when horses move around it is less likely that the trailer will be rocked off. They are easy to use: the wheel to be replaced is lifted off the ground by towing its partner on the same side on to a recess on top of the wedge.

The towing vehicle's towball should be greased and, every time you hitch up, you should make sure that the trailer lights are working properly and that the lamp lenses are clean and undamaged. The breakaway cable, which is a legal requirement on a braked trailer, must be in good condition and not attached to anything on the car that may be pulled off.

Simple but important maintenance includes cleaning out the trailer every time it's used, lifting and cleaning under rubber matting regularly and checking all hinges and locks. Your trailer should be serviced and checked regularly by a recognised dealer.

Finally, whether you have a box or a trailer, make pre-drive checks before every journey and walk round before you drive off to make sure everything is in order. You could cause serious damage if, for instance, you forget to raise the fold-down steps on your horsebox – and it has been known!

▲ A breakaway cable is a legal requirement on a braked trailer and must be in good condition.

THE JOURNEY

ORGANISATION

In terms of competition, a horse will only perform well if he has a good journey. The keys to this are vehicle maintenance, as just mentioned, preparation and driving technique. Always allow plenty of time and get all your tack, equipment and any hay and feed supplies ready the day before. Take fresh water from home whenever possible, as some horses are reluctant to drink 'strange' water. You'll find more advice on keeping your horse hydrated later in this chapter.

It's a good idea to list what you need to take. Grooms who work for top riders often have checklists for each horse, because it's too easy to forget a small but important item. For security reasons, it's best not to leave your vehicle full of expensive gear overnight.

If you need to plait your horse's mane and tail, allow extra time on the day or do it the night before. Professional grooms can plait a mane in about twenty minutes, but that takes a lot of practice! If you plait the day before and feed hay from a net, leaving the forelock plait until morning will minimise the number of seeds and short pieces getting caught in the hair.

Travel kit

Protect your horse when travelling with the following:

- A comfortable, well-fitting headcollar. Leather is safest. It will break if there is an emergency and the horse gets caught up, but nylon may not and can result in injury even when the headcollar rope is tied to a breakable rope.

- Spare headcollar and lead rope.

- Spare bridle.

- If your horse tends to throw up his head, check that he is comfortable in his travelling position and, as a safeguard, use a poll guard.

- Boots or bandages.

- A tail bandage and/or tail guard.

- A rug or lightweight sheet appropriate for the conditions. Take spare rugs of different weights to account for a change in temperature.

LOADING UP

A horse who is used to travelling and has been transported considerably in the past will load without fuss. If your horse is reluctant to load, or travels badly, get expert help.

Teach a horse to load as part of his education so that his first 'proper' journeys don't come as a sudden shock. Time spent in the early days will prove a great investment. It may sound obvious, but unless you have to travel a horse who has never been handled, you need to teach him to lead before teaching him to load, as explained in Chapter 12. Doing so should make your loading task much simpler.

TIPS FOR SAFE AND EASY LOADING

- Always wear a hard hat, gloves and sensible footwear.

- Allow plenty of time and stay calm.

- Always stand to the side when lowering or raising a ramp to avoid the risk of injury if it falls.

- Using a snaffle bridle (minus the noseband) over the headcollar your horse will travel in will give you more control.

- Park the horsebox or trailer so the interior is light and inviting and your horse has safe footing. Present him straight at the ramp, not at an angle.

- Stay beside him and look ahead, not back at him.

- Always approach the ramp in walk and let him take his time as he walks on. Don't scold him for pawing the ramp, as this is his way of testing his footing.

- If travelling a single horse in a trailer without a partition, he must be on cross-ties. Some horses who don't travel well with a partition travel better when on cross-ties, as they have more room and can position themselves how they feel best.

- If the trailer partition is in place, load the horse on the right-hand side, as he will get a smoother ride when near the centre of the road than when near the curb.

- If travelling two horses in a trailer, put the heavier one on the right-hand side.

NB: The final two points above apply to UK and any other countries where you drive on the left-hand side of the road. If travelling in a country where you drive on the right, position the horses appropriately.

DRIVE TIME

Safe, considerate driving gives your horse a better journey. Don't assume that the driver does all the hard work and the horse has it easy: it's been shown that, in transit, a horse uses as much energy as when walking for the equivalent time, no matter how considerate the driver.

If you travel your horse in a trailer, you have to follow the manufacturer's travelling position for your horse. This is usually facing forward, though trailers with rear-facing positions are available. Horseboxes may allow more leeway or, if you know your horse has a preference, you can buy a horsebox to suit. Horses definitely have likes and dislikes and the only way to tell what a particular animal prefers is to remove the partitions and see which stance he adopts when given the choice.

Studies have shown that horses lose weight at a rate of about 2kg (4.4lb) per hour when travelling. Most of this is water loss, which proves how important it is to keep horses hydrated. Many competitors, especially those in the eventing world,

◀ When towing, it's important to drive smoothly and look ahead.

give their horses free access to water when travelling by fitting corner mangers filled with water. The possible risk of doing this is that water may spill and make the floor slippery, unless you have put down enough bedding to soak it up.

I would not travel a horse with water on board unless the journey was more than four hours. In any case, on very long journeys I prefer to stop and offer horses water so that they – and the people with them – can have a break. Feeding haylage or soaked hay whilst travelling also helps to keep horses hydrated.

Whether you drive a lorry or tow a trailer, remember the following:

- If you are legally entitled to drive a horsebox but have never driven anything bigger than a car, consider taking lessons from a qualified, specialist instructor. It's foolhardy to load up a horse and drive off, even if the law says you can.

- There are also qualified instructors who can teach you to tow safely. Again, it isn't safe to load up and go. You should at least practise in a safe, off-road environment and should make your road trips towing an empty trailer. Many people find reversing a trailer is challenging, so practise this off-road, too.

- Other road users may not appreciate the extra room a large vehicle or towing set-up takes or needs. You need to think ahead and, unfortunately, be prepared for other drivers to do stupid things such as cutting in front of you.

■ When you make your first driving or towing trips with a horse on board, you will notice the effect of the extra weight – and the fact that it moves! Brake and change gear smoothly and in plenty of time, corner and negotiate roundabouts slowly and remember that restricted vision means you must rely on your side mirrors much more than when driving a car.

▶ You need to make much more use of side mirrors when driving a horsebox or towing a trailer.

CARE AT COMPETITIONS

ARRIVAL AND PREPARATION

Allowing plenty of time for your journey should ensure that you arrive at a competition or training event in plenty of time. Your first task, once you've parked up, is to ensure that your horse is calm and comfortable. In warm or hot weather there is a big risk of horses over-heating and becoming dehydrated, so let down ramps and open vents as soon as possible and offer horses water.

Some horses are reluctant to drink away from home so, when possible, take water with you. Other tactics, often used by endurance riders who have to encourage horses to drink during rides, include adding apple juice or pepper-mint cordial to a bucket of water.

If you are competing your own horse, you'll know the importance of staying calm and focused. If you are assisting a competitor, you have to help them to achieve that. That may range from biting your tongue if a rider's tension shows in the form of being more abrupt than usual, to helping work out the competition venue layout and timings and warming-up a horse on the lunge and/or under saddle.

Warming-up is a skill in itself and must be tailored according to the horse's age and experience and climatic conditions on the day. A young or unfit horse may be excited to start with, but will quickly lose his fizz and become tired – so you need to find a balance between getting him physically and mentally focused and not leaving your best performance in the collecting ring. In terms of physical issues, a horse's muscles will warm up quicker in warm weather than in cold: common sense, but sometimes forgotten!

Novice horses have to get used to the competition environment and it often helps to take them to a couple of events and just ride them round to let them soak up the atmosphere. Keep out of the way of competitors and follow rules about horse and pedestrian-designated areas.

Riders and grooms need to ensure that horses stay hydrated during hard work/competition. Don't withhold water from your horse; experts now say the best practice is to offer half a bucket of water at suitable intervals whilst he is working, such as between showjumping rounds.

Riders should keep hydrated, too. Dehydration leads to slower reactions, both physically and mentally, making accidents more likely.

AFTER THE COMPETITION

Cooling down

When you've finished competing, your first priority is to cool down your horse and get him comfortable for the homeward journey. The most effective way in hot conditions is to use cold water. The most dangerous conditions for horses are a combination of heat and humidity and, in this scenario, you need to wash and walk – apply cold water, walk the horse, wash again and so on.

Research shows that horses whose temperatures register as 40 °C (104 °F) or above and who are competing in conditions of 26.5 °C (80 °F) or above are less vulnerable to heat stress, less likely to become dehydrated and will recover more quickly if cold water is used. Using cold water will not predispose a horse to 'tie up' – that's a myth!

To cool a horse safely in the conditions above, apply cold water liberally over the neck, shoulders and body. Pay particular attention to the hindquarters, to cool down the large muscles in that area. After 30 seconds of cooling, walk the horse, again for about 30 seconds, then repeat. It is important to wash and walk, because walking encourages blood flow. The process is more effective if you can carry it out in the shade.

You can stop the cooling process when the skin over the hindquarters feels cool after a period of walking and the respiratory rate has fallen to below 30 breaths per minute.

Mud and thorns

In muddy conditions, wash off the legs and – if you've been hunting or competing cross-country – check that there are no injuries. Be especially careful if there is a risk of penetration injuries from thorns. Any thorns should be removed, taking care not to break off the point, and the site treated with appropriate wound management. If it is on or near a joint, it's worth getting your vet to check it. Keep an eye on the site and if there is any heat or swelling, veterinary attention is a must. This sort of injury, particularly when blackthorns are to blame, can cause serious lameness.

Staying away from home

Whenever possible, I try to take horses home each day, as I feel that as long as they are travelled correctly, this is less stressful for them than staying in strange stables. When it is necessary to stable away from home, be prepared to stay with a horse for as long as it takes him to settle.

Sadly, you also need to be aware of security. There have been instances of thieves targeting showgrounds overnight to steal rugs off horses' backs, along with headcollars and other valuable equipment. There have also been alleged doping incidents.

HOME AGAIN

When you get home, check the horse over again in a good light, pick out his feet and remove any dried mud and sweat stains and rug him up appropriately. Thermal rugs are particularly useful in all but hot weather and help to ensure that a horse stays warm and dry and does not break out (start sweating again after he had been cooled down). If it's too warm to use one, a lightweight fleece rug can be useful. If appropriate, use stable bandages over padding, or suitable leg wraps to add warmth and support.

Make sure he has plenty of water and a full net of hay or haylage. This will help him to relax and will also ensure that his digestive system is working properly. If he's cool and calm, feed as normal. Ignore the old tradition of giving a horse who has worked hard a bran mash (see Chapter 5) – he needs his normal feed. Leave him to eat in peace and check him later to make sure that he is relaxed and has not broken out. If he has, you may need to change his rugs and, if necessary, walk him in hand.

If a horse or pony lives out all the time and has sweated up in cold weather, using a lightweight thermal rug whilst you travel home will hopefully mean that he is dry – or drier – when you arrive. In mild weather, when he wouldn't wear a turnout rug, the best practice is to turn him out as usual so that he can roll, move around and graze. If it's cold and he's used to wearing a turnout rug, stable him with a haynet and a rug that promotes drying off if a stable is available. If it isn't – or if he doesn't like being stabled – use a breathable turnout rug that can be put on a damp or wet horse. He, like the stabled horse, should be checked later to ensure that he is comfortable. It may be necessary to wash down a horse with warm water and walk him round to cool down before rugging him for the night, whether he lives in or out.

KEY POINTS

- Be aware of horse transport legislation.
- Always carry a horse's passport when transporting him, no matter how short the journey.
- Read any relevant horsebox, trailer and tow car manuals.
- Check all vehicles before any journey.
- Muck out trailers and horseboxes after every journey.
- Be diligent about routine maintenance and professional servicing.
- Keep horses hydrated.

CHAPTER 12

On the Ground

Horse management isn't just about feeding, grooming and so on, vital though these are. Work on the ground – correct leading, loose-schooling, lungeing and long-reining – are skills that riders and non-riders alike should be proficient in. Done correctly, they can help you build fitness, muscle tone and balance.

Working a horse on the ground allows you to see the way he moves when he isn't influenced or encumbered by a rider's weight. It also allows you to influence his way of going and you'll find that a horse who improves on the ground also improves under saddle, provided, of course, that the rider is competent.

I discovered the real value of groundwork when I had a bad accident in which I broke my neck and was unable to ride for several months. I had always used loose-schooling, lungeing and long-reining when backing young horses, but I discovered that they also had enormous value when helping established horses maintain their way of going and even make progress. I'm not claiming I've discovered something new – after all, the Spanish Riding School has used in-hand work for centuries – but those of us who are first and foremost riders tend to underestimate its value.

LEADING QUESTIONS

Leading a horse is one of the first things everyone has to learn. We can all do it – or can we?

Foals are taught to lead by being encouraged to follow their dams, so unless you have a totally unhandled horse, the basics should be in place. If you are dealing with an unhandled horse, you need to tailor the approach to the individual. For instance, in some cases you will be able to use food to get the horse to follow you into a large stable without too many problems and start accustoming him to being handled from there. In others, you will have to start off in the open.

I've had all sorts of horses sent to me for backing and I can say that an unhandled or barely handled youngster can be far easier to deal with than one who is 'well handled' to the point of being spoilt! Young, uneducated horses are usually naturally curious and will come to you to investigate, so it doesn't take long to get them to accept being touched. However, those who have been petted and stuffed with titbits so they have learned to become pushy and dominant are far more difficult to deal with.

Working with a frightened or feral animal is a specialist area outside the remit of this book and if you have such a horse I strongly recommend getting help from someone who follows a humane approach and has a good reputation. One piece of advice I would pass on is that charities who carry out rescue and rehabilitation work say that, when possible, one experienced person should work with a horse during his first stages of acclimatisation to handling. The horse becomes used to and takes security from that person's voice and once the handler has established the basic lessons, the horse can move on to carrying them out with other people.

As a show producer, I need my horses to walk out when I am standing just in front of their shoulder, trot calmly in hand, halt and stand quietly. I also want them to step forward or back when asked and to move over in the stable. It doesn't take long to teach a horse to lead correctly and it isn't difficult to keep up the good work, but some people then allow themselves to get sloppy about it.

Successful in-hand show producers insist that their horses always walk out in an energetic way, halt as soon as the handler stops and stand quietly until asked to move on, whether they are in the ring or being led to the field. It's a principle we should all follow; after all, if you expect your horse to pay attention one day, then allow him to slop along at the end of a rope behind you the next, you shouldn't be surprised if he doesn't always co-operate.

The two basic leading problems are flipsides of the same coin. One is the horse who is reluctant to go forward and the other is the horse who likes to set his own pace, perhaps to the extent that he tows his would-be handler along.

If a horse is reluctant to step out, or to go into trot when asked, you may be advised to practise by leading him alongside a fence and tapping him at the girth with a schooling whip to encourage him to go forward. There is nothing wrong with using a schooling whip as an aid – though it must be used to touch or tap, not hit – and all my horses accept me carrying one and using it. The problem with using it in this scenario is that as soon as you move away from the support of the fence, most horses will swing their quarters away.

I've found that what works better is to ask a helper to use a lunge line fastened to the offside bit ring, rather like a single long-rein. Lead the horse as normal and, if he doesn't walk or trot out when asked, use the lunge line to tap him on the side and, at the same time, prevent his quarters from swinging out. With this system, he doesn't associate the correction with the person who is leading him.

The horse must be used to the feel of a lunge line along his side before you try this approach. If he is unbroken or you don't know his past schooling history, introduce the idea as explained in the long-reining section later in this chapter.

The horse who sets off at his own pace must be taught to respond to body language and to pressure and release. Work in a small arena or round pen if possible, using either an ordinary headcollar or a training/pressure headcollar which acts on the nose. Some have a sliding strap that runs across the nose and others are made from rope. You may need to use a longer than usual headcollar rope or a lunge line.

Ask the horse to move on and, if he tries to tow you along, give a short, sharp pull on the lead rope. As soon as he reacts by coming back to you or halting, release the pressure, praise him quietly and walk off again. It may take a few repetitions, but he will learn that if he pays attention to you rather than following his own agenda, life is much more pleasant.

You can, of course, lead an onward-bound horse using a bridle, but hanging on to his mouth won't give you any more control – and yanking on the bit rings will make things worse.

LOOSE-SCHOOLING

Over the past few years, round pens have become the 'must have' on many yards. They provide an excellent environment not only for loose-schooling but for riding newly backed youngsters, as they allow a horse to go forward but at the same time, keep calm. They also encourage him to bend on a circle.

I've always found that horses love working loose in round pens. They look on it as playtime but, done correctly, it also helps develop their balance and rhythm. The emphasis is on doing it correctly: chasing a horse with a lunge whip is not loose-schooling. I may use a lunge whip, but – as when lungeing – the key is to influence a horse with your stance, body language and voice.

Position yourself behind his girth line to encourage him forwards and in front of it to slow him down. I use voice commands a lot, as I find horses are incredibly receptive to vocal tone. If you use an encouraging, upbeat tone, the horse will naturally go forward, whilst giving a command in a soothing, 'down-hill' tone will influence him to come back a gear.

If possible, I use a helper who understands the way I work when loose-schooling, but you can work alone. You must stay alert and be quick on your feet, because although a horse will do everything he can to avoid running you over, he can't help it if you get in his way! If there are two of you, it's even more important to keep your wits about you.

The other benefit of loose-schooling in a round pen is that you can see whether a horse finds it easier to work on one rein than on the other. Most do – and loose-schooling and correct lungeing can help develop suppleness. You can also loose-school before riding; I like to tack up a horse in a snaffle bridle and use the bridle reins as an alternative to side-reins, adjusting them according to how I want to influence his way of going.

I find this means you can tack up, loose-school, then move straight into ridden work. You're not rushing the horse, but it does save time on a busy yard. If I want to encourage a lowering of the head and neck and lifting of the back, I lower the stirrup irons to jumping length, unfasten the centre buckle of the reins and pass the reins through the irons, fastening the centre buckle under the belly (see photo on page 170). If I want to keep a light but not restricting connection with the horse's mouth, I run the stirrups up the leathers, secure them and pass the reins behind the irons, as shown in the next picture.

Loose-schooling over poles and small fences is something I do with every horse, even those who aren't expected to jump as part of their competition regimes. It encourages them to flex their joints and step through behind and they all seem to enjoy it. Loose-jumping is excellent for the horse who doesn't have a naturally good canter, because it helps him to learn to step through from behind.

Loose-schooling over poles on the ground which are set at the correct distances *for that particular horse* encourages a horse to flex his joints without imposing too much stress. Again, this also helps to improve his balance; set on a curve round the diameter of a round pen they make him think more carefully about where he puts his feet.

◀ Loose-schooling over poles on the ground which are set at the correct distances for that particular horse encourages him to flex his joints without imposing too much stress.

LUNGEING

Whilst loose-schooling will help a horse find and establish his balance, lungeing will help him use that balance in a way that translates to ridden work. A lot of people underestimate lungeing by looking on it purely as a way to exercise a horse when they haven't got time to ride, or to take the edge off a sharp animal before they get on. However, you can use it to improve your horse's way of going quite dramatically, which will have enormous benefits for his ridden work. When a horse learns to go correctly without a rider, he finds ridden work easier, as work on the lunge will help build the correct muscles. It will also help build his confidence.

I am sometimes sent horses to school who arrive with a history of problems, or who find aspects of their work difficult. My own horses don't always find it plain sailing – for instance, cobs and other heavier types often have rhythmic trots but find canter under saddle difficult. In this sort of scenario, I will spend several weeks working a horse loose and then on the lunge to get him physically capable of what I'm asking and to give him balance and confidence without a rider. A horse can only be in self-carriage and give a good ride if he has the muscles in the right place to do so!

Lungeing is hard work for a horse, so don't overdo it. With a young horse who hasn't built up fitness, 5 minutes on each rein, working in walk and trot, may be enough to start with. With a fit, established horse, you may be working for a total of 20–30 minutes. As when schooling under saddle, always work on both reins to avoid the horse becoming one-sided. Most horses find it easier to work on one rein than the other and, when riding or working from the ground, I prefer to start off on the more difficult rein, though I know some trainers disagree. To me, it makes more sense to ask the horse to carry out more difficult work when he has more energy.

I lunge to help improve a horse's way of going rather than for exercise and for that reason, I lunge from the bit. If I need to exercise a horse from the ground, I loose-school in a round pen; if you don't have that facility and need to lunge a horse who is cutting teeth, it's sensible to use a lunge cavesson.

There are many types of lungeing equipment, from side-reins to systems using cords and pulleys. Different trainers have different preferences, but I prefer to work just with one or two lunge reins. As explained in the next section, I adjust the way I clip the lunge rein to the bit rings according to the way I want to influence the horse's way of going and have found that for me, this is the best way of making sure that corrections on the lunge carry over into ridden work.

Whatever equipment you use, you must be able to influence the horse through your voice and stance. The textbook way of lungeing is to stand still and pivot on the spot whilst you encourage the horse to circle around you, but it's more effective to stand closer to the horse and walk a small circle. If you want him to go forwards, you need to be positioned at an angle slightly behind the girth. Stepping forwards so you are in front of the girth will encourage him to slow down or stop and stepping towards him will encourage him to move out. Use the lunge whip as an extension of your arm, but don't wave it around aimlessly and never use it to hit a horse.

At the same time, use your voice in an energetic or calming way, as appropriate. It doesn't matter what verbal cue you give, as it isn't what you say but the way you say it – however, it's prudent to be consistent. Don't keep up a constant stream of dialogue or tongue clicks, or your horse will just switch off.

I've learned that it's important to teach a horse to stand quietly during lungeing sessions as well as to go forward. If you start him straight off on a circle, it tends to make him anxious, especially if he is naturally that way inclined. Some horses will go into automatic pilot mode and although they seem to be working obediently, they aren't actually listening to you and waiting to learn what you want them to do.

When I start a lungeing session I always spend a little time just standing with the horse, adjusting tack, watching other people working, or just having a chat. That way, he doesn't get anxious about his work and learns to wait and find out what I want him to do rather than making assumptions.

My horses also learn to wait, either in the school or the round pen, whilst I'm adjusting poles or fences. It all has a knock-on effect of helping them accept that there are times when they have to stand still and stay calm and relaxed. In turn, this pays dividends when they have to stand and wait at a competition, on a hack or in the hunting field. Everything you do with your horse on the ground will reflect in his ridden work, so the more you can build his trust, confidence and respect, the better.

LUNGEING EQUIPMENT

There is a wide variety of equipment that can be used when lungeing, from basic side-reins to training aids designed to encourage a horse to work in an outline. All trainers have their likes, dislikes and opinions; for instance, some like to use plain side-reins because they believe that they encourage a horse to work into a contact, whilst others prefer elasticated ones because they feel that it's better to have a slight amount of give. A lot of people are enthusiastic about and get good results from training aids which fasten round the quarters as well as to the bit.

I won't say I would never use a particular piece of equipment, as long as it has a humane and logical action, but I've worked out my own system through watching and working hundreds of horses of all ages and types. I rarely use side-reins because to my eye, when they are fastened to the girth or the side rings of a roller, they can block a horse's movement rather than encourage him to move freely.

However, if you want to use them, they should be fastened loosely when you are allowing the horse to warm up and then, when you are ready to work, adjusted so that there is a light contact when the horse is standing in a normal working frame, with his nose just in front of the vertical.

One occasion when I do use side-reins is if I have a horse to back or school who has issues with a bit. In this situation, I will do his early loose-schooling work using a headcollar and attach side-reins to its side rings. This gives him the idea of working within a frame, but without putting any pressure on his mouth and, once he's happy with this, the side-reins can be attached to the bit rings.

I never stand a horse in a stable with fixed side-reins. I know some trainers do this because they feel it helps to get a horse to work naturally in a round outline, but I believe there is a risk that this will make him stiff and sore and also encourage him to come behind the bit.

Never have side-reins – or any other equipment – adjusted so that you are forcing a horse into a particular outline, whether you are working him on the lunge or under saddle. It's far better to do things in small steps than to try to

◄ Attaching side-reins to the side rings of a headcollar or lunge cavesson gives a horse the idea or working within a frame without putting pressure on his mouth.

do too much in one go. In the long run, doing it a step at the time is quicker, because if you ask too much, too soon, the horse is more likely to resist and panic. Undoing mistakes is far more difficult and time-consuming than having a little patience the first time round and, if the learning process is made as pleasant as possible, your horse will be more receptive to new experiences and will enjoy his work.

Although it's important to make sure that horses are comfortable in their mouths, a lot of resistance which appears to be linked to the bit is actually rooted elsewhere. For instance, a horse might hang his tongue out the side of his mouth because the bit is the wrong shape or thickness for his mouth conformation, but it might be that he finds it difficult to adopt a particular posture and mouth resistances are a reaction to a problem that actually has nothing to do with the bit.

Mouth resistances such as teeth-grinding or putting the tongue out to one side are often linked to tension and can become habitual. I had one horse who habitually stuck out his tongue, but the more established he became in his work, the less frequently he did it. He became a lovely ride, accepted a double bridle and won the retrained racehorses' final at the Horse of the Year Show.

I always lunge using a snaffle bridle, a cotton web lunge line that is comfortable to hold and a standard lunge whip, holding the lunge rein in the hand nearest to the horse and the lunge whip in the other: so if I'm lungeing on the left rein, I have the lunge rein in my left hand. You should think of keeping an elastic contact on the lunge rein, aiming for a similar feeling to when you are riding. Keep your elbow bent so that you don't tighten the muscles of your arm and, in so doing, create a fixed hold. This is especially important when you lunge from the bit. If the horse is soft in your hand, you are doing it correctly and if he's strong, you are doing it wrong!

It doesn't matter whether you hold the lunge line in loops or fold it back and forward across the palm of your hand, but never wrap it round your hand in an attempt to anchor a strong horse, or you could be badly injured.

LUNGEING FROM SCRATCH

Most horses are taught to lunge as part of the backing process, but if you're starting from scratch and don't have a round pen, you'll find it easier if you close off part of a large school with jump stands and poles so you have a smaller area to work in. Build the jumps high enough to discourage the horse from jumping out, but so that they will knock down if he tries to do so.

Some trainers like to teach a horse to lunge working solo, starting by leading him round and reinforcing the vocal commands to halt and walk on. They then move gradually further away from the horse. Others use a helper at the horse's head, but if you use this system, it's important that the helper is there purely for back-up and must not give any vocal commands. You want the horse to focus on you, not be distracted by your helper.

I like a helper to be on the outside of the horse, not between me and the horse. My method is to ask a helper to hold a lead rein connected to the bit and to stand still when I ask the horse to halt, and walk on when I ask the horse to do the same. I only ever do this in walk and trot and you and the helper need to be very careful in trot, as there's always a chance that when a horse goes forward into the gait, he will buck or kick out.

Another method I sometimes use if I want to teach a horse on my own is to start off in a very large stable or a tiny courtyard. However I do it, I make sure that the horse is confident with me holding a lunge whip and happy for me to move it around near him before I start lungeing proper.

Some people might think I'm over-cautious in all the precautions I take, but to me, it's simply common sense to think ahead. Being aware of what could happen allows you to introduce new experiences in small steps, which is what training should always be about.

LUNGEING FOR IMPROVEMENT

In my lungeing system, there are four different set-ups: one to encourage the horse to stretch his topline, two to encourage more flexion and one to correct a horse who falls out through the outside shoulder.

When I'm working a horse loose or lungeing him and want him to stretch his topline, I tack him up using a snaffle bridle, an ordinary pair of reins and the horse's saddle. I run the stirrup irons down the leathers, then undo the centre buckle of the reins, pass each half of the rein through a stirrup iron and knot them together at the girth. The lunge rein is clipped to the inside bit ring. It can be beneficial to work a horse this way for a brief period on each rein before you get on him and, because he's already tacked up, it's quick and easy to change from lungeing to riding. It also helps encourage the 'peacocky' horse who naturally goes with a higher than ideal head-carriage (which automatically means he has a flat, tight back and doesn't use his hind legs and hindquarters properly) to work in a longer, lower outline.

This set-up allows the horse to open up his movement, lift his back and stretch over his topline, but there is enough leeway to ensure that he is not restricted too much. If he raises his head too high, the signal via the bit asks him to lower it again and, as soon as he does so, the pressure is released – so he is rewarded instantly for doing the right thing. I've found that horses take kindly to working this way and that it encourages them to make nice transitions, using their back ends and not putting their heads in the air.

To encourage more flexion to the inside, pass the lunge rein through the inside bit ring, then clip it to the girth buckle. If you want him to carry his head and neck a little higher, pass the lunge rein through the inside bit ring, but clip it to the D-ring on the front of the saddle. To encourage him to come up in front

◄ ▲ Using this set-up allows you to work a horse for a brief period on each rein before you get on him and makes it quick and easy to change from lungeing to riding.

a little more whilst asking for flexion, clip the lunge rein to the saddle D-ring on the outside.

A lot of horses fall through their outside shoulder and I've found the best way to correct this is to pass the lunge rein through the inside bit ring, then take it over the horse's head and clip it to the outside D-ring. This gives the same effect as asking for a little flexion, but using the outside rein to prevent him falling out through the shoulder when you are riding.

Watch your horse whilst you are working him and, if necessary, adjust the set-up. You might find that you need to work him in one position for a few minutes to start with, then adjust it.

▶ To encourage more flexion to the inside, pass the lunge rein through the inside bit ring, then clip it to the girth buckle. To encourage the horse to come up more in front, clip it to the saddle D-ring as shown by the dotted line.

◀ A good way to teach the horse not to fall out through the outside shoulder is to pass the lunge rein through the inside bit ring, then take it over the horse's head and clip it to the outside D-ring.

WORKING ON THE LUNGE

Most lunge work is carried out in trot, but I also use it to teach canter transitions. When I'm backing horses, or re-schooling one who has come to me with problems, I don't canter under saddle until the horse is cantering happily on the lunge, on both reins. Technique is important, because you mustn't hurry a horse into canter – or through any other transition. As when riding, you need to warn him that you are going to ask him to do something different.

I like to relate the commands I use for lungeing to those I use for riding. It's usually more difficult for a horse to keep his balance in canter on the lunge than in trot, as there is more momentum, so when you ask for a transition to canter it's important not to hassle the horse. I squeeze the lunge rein to warn him I'm going to ask him to do something – the equivalent of squeezing with my inside hand to give a half-halt when riding – and use the voice command.

LONG-REINING

At one time, long-reining was a traditional part of every horse's or pony's education. These days, it's sometimes looked on as old-fashioned but when it's done properly, it can be of great benefit to the ridden horse.

For a start, it can be a stepping stone in the backing process, as you can use it to teach a young horse to start, stop and steer before you get on him. It can also be a good way to exercise a pony when there is no one available small enough to ride him, or simply as a way of adding variety to work.

There are two forms of long-reining. One is where the horse is in front of you, which for the sake of clarity I call driving. The other way is to long-rein on a circle, which some people refer to as double-lungeing. Here, the inside rein comes directly to the handler's inside hand and the outside rein goes around the horse's quarters and back to the handler's outside hand – so if the horse is on the left rein, the inside rein clips to the left bit ring and goes directly to your left hand, whilst the right rein goes around the horse and is held in your right hand.

Because I use the lungeing set-ups explained earlier, I tend to use the driving method. A proficient handler can use it to help educate a horse's mouth, as a combination of voice commands and gentle rein signals teaches him to answer rein aids without the added complication of a rider's weight, and you can also teach him to flex and bend correctly by using your inside and outside reins as you would when riding.

Long-reining teaches a horse to go forwards and straight confidently, which will also be reflected in his ridden work, and helps build up his muscles. If you're a parent coping with a small pony, long-reining will give him enough exercise to keep him ticking over when children are unable to ride and, if the pony is a good doer, will help you keep his weight at the right level. As an added bonus, you could find that you've also become fitter!

TIPS AND TECHNIQUES

If you haven't long-reined before, try to find someone accomplished to show you how to do it. It isn't rocket science, but you have to be aware of the risks of putting too much pressure on the horse's mouth. If necessary, introduce it by long-reining from a headcollar or a bitless bridle that acts only on the nose, not on the poll. Don't use a German hackamore with long shanks, as it can exert powerful leverage.

Whether you are using a standard bridle and bit or a bitless set-up, remember that, because you are a long way away from the horse's head, there is the potential to exert greater pressure on the mouth or nose even without realising it. When I'm working with a young horse, I prefer to use a rubber or 'plastic' bit, either jointed or unjointed, rather than a metal one, as I feel it's kinder on the horse's mouth. When you're long-reining, your hands are lower than when you are riding and the bit has a more direct, downwards action on the horse's mouth. I carry the lunge reins or long-reins in the same position as when riding.

Again, as when riding, you must have a light, soft contact with the horse's mouth so it's important to keep your elbows bent so that you have soft arms and, as a result, soft hands. If your arms become straight, the muscles tighten and you lose sensitivity and 'feel'.

It's important to stay safe. Some horses are not bothered by the feel sensation of the long-reins going along or behind their body, but others find it worrying to begin with and even the kindest may kick out in response. Introduce the reins one at a time in safe surroundings, moving them gently

▲ A 'plastic' bit with a central metal core for safety is kind on a young horse's mouth when long-reining.

along the horse's body until he accepts them. Always wear a hard hat, gloves and safe, comfortable footwear and make sure you stand out of kicking range.

Always long-rein in a safe environment and start off in an enclosed space. To begin with, I have a helper at the horse's head, with a lead rope clipped to the inside bit ring. As with lungeing, the helper is there as back-up and does not give any vocal commands, simply walking on and stopping as I direct the horse.

When I start long-reining without a helper, I let the long-reins hang loose at the horse's sides. This way, it's easier to sort things out if he does whip round. An experienced handler can usually prevent this happening, but occasionally, you'll find that you're facing the wrong end of the horse. If this happens, don't panic. Simply drop one of the long-reins, walk calmly up to the horse, coiling the line as you go, then sort out the other one and carry on as if nothing had happened.

As the horse progresses and becomes more confident, I tack him up with the stirrups let down to a short riding length and pass the long-reins through the irons. This prevents the long-reins slipping down his sides and helps to keep him straight when working on straight lines. I long-rein in trot as well as in walk.

Even as you and the horse gain experience, retain the practice of long-reining only in a safe environment. I'm lucky and have access to quiet tracks, so I might long-rein a horse round tracks and fields as well as in the school. However, I wouldn't long-rein on roads where I was likely to meet a lot of traffic and, if I go out on quiet roads, I like to have an escort.

KEY POINTS

- Loose-schooling teaches a horse to find his balance and rhythm; lungeing teaches him to use those attributes in a way that translates to ridden work.

- When lunge or long-reins are attached to a bit, it must be some form of simple snaffle. Never long-rein using any type of curb bit or any snaffle with a lever action, as this would put too much pressure on the horse's mouth.

- Teach a horse to stand quietly on the lunge or long-reins as well as to go forward.

- Introduce long-reins in the stable so the horse gets used to the sensation of them against his sides.

- Long-rein only in a safe environment.

- When doing groundwork, always wear a hard hat and gloves and, if long-reining on quiet roads or on tracks where you are likely to meet vehicles or dog walkers, wear high-vis clothing so that you can be seen easily.

- A horse should wear boots when being lunged or loose-schooled.

CHAPTER 13

Fit for the Job

All horses and ponies, whether they be top-level competition horses or used for everyday hacking, must be fit *for the jobs they are asked to do* if they are to perform well and stay sound. Getting a horse fit is a science and an art, but also requires common sense and observation. It's the owner and/or carer who has to decide whether, for instance, a horse is too fat or too thin, or needs his saddle adjusting to be able to work comfortably.

So what does fitness mean? An excellent definition of a fit horse is given by competition horse specialist vet Andy Bathe as 'one who can do the job expected of him without undue stress'.

Many – perhaps most – horses get fit enough to cope with their work-load, including lower levels of competition, through the normal mix of hacking and schooling which comprises the average regime. However, true fitness – as opposed to being able to cope with a workload – demands fitness-specific exercise.

A horse who is at peak fitness for one discipline will not necessarily be able to cope with a different workload. For instance, a horse who can complete a 100km (60-mile) endurance ride would not necessarily cope with activities demanding intermittent periods of high-intensity exercise such as polo or showjumping. The same applies to human athletes: a champion marathon runner probably wouldn't win a 100-metre sprint.

Nor can you assume that a fit horse is a well-schooled horse. In fact, he could be super-fit but be as supple as a plank! This is why exercise to build and maintain fitness should be built into a schedule alongside training to develop suppleness and responsiveness.

You can't maintain peak fitness all the time and the greater the demands placed on a horse, the more important this becomes. At top level, riders know they have certain competitions for which they will aim to bring a horse into peak fitness, followed by periods when work is eased off and the horse is kept 'ticking over'. For instance, an event rider will plan a four-star horse's competition year aiming, perhaps, to have him at peak fitness for Badminton and Burghley.

We also know that it's possible to have a horse too fit, though in practical terms, this is much rarer than having him not fit enough. The danger of over-fittening is that you are putting too much stress on a horse; eventually, this will take its toll, particularly on joints and tendons.

◀ Horses must be fit for specific jobs and an endurance horse would not necessarily be fit enough for showjumping or eventing.

FITTENING GUIDELINES

Certain guidelines apply whatever discipline the horse is aimed at.

■ A younger horse or one who has never been got fit before will take longer to reach the appropriate level than one who has. Give young horses time – TBs may be racing fit as 2- and 3-year-olds, but they are very different from, say, native ponies, Warmbloods or Irish Draughts. They are also managed differently and, it has to be said, do not necessarily stay sound. The 'wastage rate' in Flat racing is high and whilst point-to-pointers and National Hunt horses hopefully have longer racing careers, they are usually given more time to mature before being put into full training.

■ A horse who is given an extended time off will take longer to come back to fitness than one who is given several short breaks, or kept in light work. At one time, hunters were traditionally turned out to grass at the end of the season, then brought up at the beginning of August to start fittening work. Now, more riders taper off their hunters' workload at the end of the season and keep them in work, whether that be hacking or competing, through the summer.

■ If you have to (or decide to) give a fit horse time off work, he should retain most of his fitness for about two months provided he is turned out. A horse on box rest will, as common sense suggests, lose fitness more quickly.

▥ When you exercise a horse to improve his fitness, you are by definition putting him under stress. This isn't a bad thing, but is essential; gradually, his body will adapt and he will become able to cope, whether you are at the stage of asking him to trot for 10 or 20 minutes. The scientific name for this is progressive loading. The important word is *progressive*. If you ask too much, too soon, you will overload rather than load the horse's body, which will probably result in injury. Ideally, increase the intensity of exercise every two to three weeks but, if in doubt, ask for smaller increases in effort over a longer period than you had originally planned.

▥ When working a horse – whether you're exercising or schooling – it's just as important to cool down as it is to warm up. In simple terms, reverse the order of your warm-up, so if you started by walking for 5 minutes and followed with 5 minutes of trotting, cool down by working in trot for 5 minutes and finish with 5 minutes in walk. Follow the same rule whatever you are doing, even if you are 'just' hacking. There is a lot to be said for the classic advice, 'Walk the first mile out and the last mile back.' In practical terms, it might be difficult advice to follow when you're riding a lively youngster on a cold day, but do try. This is where a horse-walker can be so useful, as horses rarely mess around on one and it provides a safe way of warming up.

◀ It is as important to cool down your horse as it is to warm him up, whether you are exercising or schooling.

▥ Don't be discouraged when the rate of increase in fitness slows down as you work through your programme. This is normal; you will usually see a marked improvement quickly, but the fitter the horse becomes, the less noticeable the improvement will be.

■ The oft-quoted advice that roadwork 'hardens' tendons has yet to be proved. Trotting on roads puts concussion through the limbs – as, of course, does working on any hard ground. However, some trainers like to trot up hills. Their theory, which sounds plausible, is that this encourages the horse to use his hind legs and means that less weight is taken on the forelegs.

■ Riders should pay attention to their own fitness as well as that of their horses. An unfit rider is insecure in the saddle and slower to react, which increases the risk of accidents.

■ Ideally, horses should be in good condition but not overweight at the start of a fitness programme. In some cases, that isn't possible; if you buy or are sent an overweight horse and need to get him fit, walk exercise and a sensible eating plan (see Chapter 5) will work together to kick-start a fitness programme.

■ Pay attention to the fit of your tack; in particular, the fit of your saddle. There is more information about this in the next chapter, but a horse can change shape drastically throughout a fitness programme, through losing weight and/or building up muscle. You will need to have his saddle adjusted or, if you have sufficient knowledge, use numnahs and/or pads to rebalance it.

■ Some experts say that competitions will not, in themselves, get horses fit. However, as they constitute discipline-specific work, they must surely play a useful part. Depending on the level of competition, it can be introduced during or at the end of stage 4 in the fitness programme guidelines below.

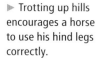

▶ Trotting up hills encourages a horse to use his hind legs correctly.

FITNESS PROGRAMMES

There is no single way of getting a horse fit, only general principles, as outlined above. Ask five top event riders how they get their horses fit for competition and you'll probably get five different answers, albeit with common strategies! For instance, if you live in a hilly area, you'll be able to use hill work to underline your regime. If you live in a part of the UK where you see nothing larger than a molehill, you'll probably use a form of interval training, as explained later in this chapter.

It's impossible to give a definite timescale for taking a horse from unfit to being fit enough to, say, cope with a Pre-novice event, but most experts seem to agree that twelve weeks is realistic. This allows ten weeks for building fitness plus an extra two weeks for problems that you or your horse may encounter.

A SUGGESTED SCHEDULE

It can be very annoying to hear scientists say that there's no such thing as a standard fitness programme. That might be true, but you have to work to some sort of schedule! The easiest way is to divide it into four stages and make sure that your horse is coping well at each level before moving on to the next.

Stage 1

The basis of any fitness programme for any type of horse or pony is long, slow distance work (LSD.) This will mean between two and four weeks of walk work, starting with half-hour periods and gradually building up through an hour to an hour and a half. It may be necessary and even sensible to do the very early stages in an arena or field; some unfit horses are sluggish but others are silly and it isn't safe to hack out on one who thinks fitness work should be enlivened by airs above the ground. If you have to lunge a horse before it's safe to get on him, keep it to the minimum and keep your circles as large as possible.

If you have access to a horse-walker, you can count your blessings – but you can't use it as a total replacement for walk work under saddle. Weight-loading is part of the regime and whilst work on a walker or even long-reining can help, working with the added weight of a rider on board helps build bone strength.

Keep a good quality of walk. It should be active and rhythmical, though not hurried. The horse does not have to be truly on the bit, but should be what racehorse trainers call 'on the bridle', stepping into a contact without leaning on the rider's hands.

▲ Schooling figures can be used to build suppleness.

Be aware that some horses, particularly young ones, can suddenly run out of fuel, even in walk. In this situation, be prepared to get off and walk alongside him, if it's safe to do so.

Stage 2

Once your horse is comfortable with an hour's walk exercise per day, you can step up to the next stage. You can be more precise about walking large figures such as 20m circles, three-loop serpentines and changes of rein and, if your horse has reached the required stage of schooling, introduce loops, leg-yielding, shoulder-in and rein-back to build suppleness.

At this stage, you can also introduce short periods of trot, aiming for a balanced, rhythmical working trot. If you live in a hilly area, trotting up gradual inclines will encourage the horse to use his hind legs.

Lungeing in walk and trot can be introduced to your regime, working equally on both reins. Build up gradually, starting with 5–10 minutes on each rein and again keeping circles as large as possible.

Stage 3

You should now be able to introduce short periods of canter work. It's important – as always – that this should be on good going, but whilst you should avoid ground that is too deep, rock-hard or has a slippery surface over hard going, you should be aiming to work over different types of terrain.

Whilst I canter my horses on the lunge and find lungeing a good way of improving canter transitions, I don't like to do it for long periods. Constant circle work imposes strain on the joints, particularly the hock joints, and cantering under saddle allows you greater control.

If control becomes a matter for discussion, you may need to re-think the tack you use. With some horses, a high-ring Grakle noseband makes all the difference. Not only does it discourage the horse from opening his mouth too wide and crossing his jaw to try to evade the rider, it is more comfortable for young horses who are cutting teeth, as it doesn't put any pressure on the cheek teeth.

In general, I don't use training aids, but I do find that a correctly fitted Market Harborough can be valuable, as explained in the next chapter.

Pole work is especially useful at this stage, mentally and physically. For some reason, riders who don't want to jump often assume that they don't need to work their horses over poles on the ground. Pupils at my showing clinics are often surprised – and occasionally worried – when I start putting poles on the ground, but soon realise the benefits pole work brings. There is certainly nothing to worry about, as all you're doing is making it easier for the horse to use himself, as long as the poles are spaced correctly for his stride.

For horses, general guidelines are:

Walk poles – 90 cm (3 ft).

Trot poles – 1.2–1.35 m (4 ft–4 ft 6 in).

Canter poles – When schooling, I use a distance of 3.65 m (12 ft) because this is the distance showjumping course-builders work to.

Distances will need to be adjusted for ponies and for horses with particularly long or short strides.

Stage 4

If in doubt whether your horse is ready to move up to the final stage of a fitness programme, wait. This is where you increase the effort and the duration of work and it's better to hold back and consolidate work for a further week than ask for too much, too soon.

Three or four schooling sessions per week can be combined with hacking, work over poles on the ground, gridwork over small fences and trotting and cantering uphill on good going. Working over poles on the ground with alternate raised ends will increase the effort required. Longer canter sessions will help build cardiovascular fitness.

INTERVAL TRAINING

Most riders will be able to gauge their horse's fitness by his performance, but if you need a more structured approach, look at interval training. This can also be the best system for those who do not have access to hills.

The basis of interval training, whether for human or equine athletes, is that set work periods are carried out over a specific time, with intervals at walk to allow for partial recovery. It should be started when you reach the end of Stage 4 in the general fitness programme above and incorporated into your other work; general advice is that it should be done every four days. To give you some parameters, six weeks of interval training should see most horses capable of competing in a BE80 event, but it will take three and a half to four months to reach a level commensurate with that demanded by an Advanced three-day event.

There are pros and cons to interval training: the main advantage is that you can make structured increases in work, but because the periods of effort are short, there is less risk of injury and fatigue. Against that, horses get to learn what happens next and anticipation of canter work can lead to some becoming excited.

Many riders use a form of interval training without really defining it as such. For example, if you include hill work sessions in which you repeatedly trot uphill and walk down, you are doing interval training.

For interval training proper, you need to work at specific speeds of trot and canter, which you can work out by establishing a work area or areas of 400m (440 yards) on good going. An all-weather gallop provides the perfect environment, but most of us have to be content with the side of a field. You will also need a stopwatch to time both your horse's speed over your marked distances and his pulse and respiratory rates in recovery. Serious competitors, particularly endurance riders, often use heart monitors, which allow them to check their horses' heart rates without dismounting.

▼ If the going is suitable, you can use the side of a field for an interval training regime.

You should aim to establish an active trot that covers 220m (240 yards) per minute, which means it should take 1 minute 49 seconds to cover 400m. Unless your horse's natural stride fits these requirements, you'll need to practise to establish the speed and recognise what it feels like.

For the first session, warm up your horse in walk for 10–15 minutes, then trot for 2 minutes, walk for 3 minutes to allow a partial recovery; trot for 2 minutes, then stop and take heart and respiration rates. When you've done this, walk for another 10 minutes, then measure the rates again. This will give you a snapshot of your horse's current state of fitness – or lack of it.

As measuring recovery relies on measuring heart and respiration rates, you need to establish your horse's base rates. Approximate heart rates are:

Resting 24–42 bpm (beats per minute)

Standing ready for work 40–65 bpm

Active walk 60–80 bpm

Active trot 130–150 bpm

Canter 120–170 bpm

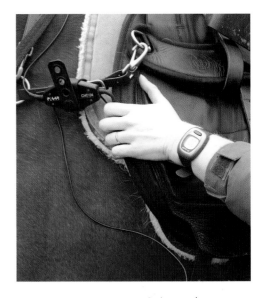

▲ Serious endurance riders often use heart monitors to check their horses' heart rates.

What you hope to achieve is that, after the final rest interval, your horse's heart rate will fall back to above but not too far above his ready-for-work base rate. You can interpret his final heart rate as follows:

100 beats per minute – he is working, but could work a bit harder.

120 – A good level to aim at: he has worked hard enough and recovered well.

150 – You have pushed him too hard for his stage of fitness and need to go back a stage.

As building fitness means building tolerance to stress, expect his heart rate after the final rest interval to be higher than 120 bpm. The respiration rate should never exceed the heart rate; if it does, stop the training session, let the horse recover and, when you start the next session, go back a stage and make sure that recovery rates are normal before moving on.

Gradually build up both the length of time you trot for and the number of repetitions. You should reach the stage where your horse can manage three sessions of trotting for 3 minutes and walking for 3 minutes, then trot for 3 minutes, halt and take the pulse and respiration rates. Finally, walk for 10 minutes and take the readings again to make sure he has recovered properly.

When you're happy with his recovery rates from the above routine, increase the length of the trot periods to 5 minutes but reduce the number of repetitions to give a pattern of:

Trot for 5 minutes, rest for 3

Trot for 5 minutes, rest for 3

Trot for 5 minutes, rest for 3

Trot for 5 minutes, halt and take pulse and respiration rates

Walk for 10 minutes, take rates again to check recovery

The final stage for most riders will be to introduce canter work. Again, you need to establish the correct speed of 350m (383 yards) per minute, which will mean riding 400m in 1 minute 8 seconds. Your next work pattern is:

Increase your warm-up period to 20 minutes in walk and trot

Canter for 1 minute 8 seconds

Trot for 3 minutes

Canter for 3 minutes, halt and take pulse and respiration rates

Walk for 10 minutes, take rates again to check recovery

When you're happy with recovery rates, build up the canter times until your pattern is:

Canter for 3 minutes

Trot for 3 minutes

Canter for 3 minutes, halt and take pulse and respiration rates

Walk for 10 minutes, take final rates

As your horse's fitness and recovery rates improve, you will feel him finding the work easier. You can then add in a third lot of canter and trot periods to give:

Canter for 3 minutes

Trot for 3 minutes

Canter for 3 minutes

Trot for 3 minutes

Canter for 3 minutes, halt and take pulse and respiration rates

Walk for 10 minutes, take final rates

At this stage, you may feel your horse is fit enough to cope with his workload and demands of competition. This will probably apply to most Riding Club competitors and to those competing in Novice dressage and lower-level show-jumping competitions. If necessary, you can take things a step further to take you up to BE90 eventing level, which requires establishing a stronger canter in which you can cover 435m (476 yards) per minute. Start with two canter periods and build up to three, as above.

Interval training might sound like fitness-by-numbers and in one way, it is. However, you should think of it as a framework that can be adapted to suit your horse, your environment and your needs.

KEY POINTS

- All horses and ponies must be fit for the job they are expected to do.

- A fit horse can be defined as 'one who can do the job expected of him without undue stress'.

- A horse who is at peak fitness for one discipline will not necessarily be able to cope with a different workload.

- The basis of any fitness programme for any type of horse or pony is long, slow distance work (LSD).

- A form of interval training may be the only option for those who do not have access to hills.

CHAPTER 14

Choosing and Fitting Tack

Choosing and using appropriate tack and fitting it correctly is part of good horse management. Despite that, it's surprising how many owners and riders who are knowledgeable and competent in many other spheres make mistakes, some of them basic and down to lack of observation and common sense as much as to lack of knowledge.

Go to any show and you'll see saddles bouncing off horses' backs or which obviously restrict an animal's movement; bits which are the wrong size and/or adjusted at the wrong height; nosebands which are too tight; stirrup irons which are the wrong size for the rider's feet; browbands which pinch a horse's ears and so on. It can be a long and depressing list and that's before you even start considering whether the equipment used is appropriate for the horse's way of going and stage of schooling and the rider's ability!

Every rider and trainer has opinions on what they like and don't like. I'm no exception and in some cases, it comes down to just that – a matter of opinion. Later in this chapter I'll explain what I use most often and why it works for me and for the horses I train, which I hope will be useful.

There are and always have been fashions in tack, but despite clever marketing, there are no magic bits that will transform your horse and no magic saddles that will turn you into, say, a Grand Prix dressage rider. At the same time, there are some bit designs which will suit your horse's mouth conformation more than others and some saddles which will help – or hinder – your position.

BITS AND BITTING

There are thousands of bits available – the snaffle family on its own runs to hundreds of designs – which tends to make riders think that bitting is a horrifically complicated subject. It can be, but only if you make it so. Be informed, but at the same time, keep it simple by remembering some basic tenets.

- A bit (or bits, if you're using a double bridle) is a means of control, but not through force.

- Some people prefer to ride bitless on a point of principle. That is, of course, their decision, but it will rule them out of some forms of competition. Also, most riders and trainers, including me, believe that you can only get true communication and finesse by using a bit. You can't get the same subtlety and responsiveness using a bitless bridle *unless* the horse has been trained to a decent level using a bit.

- It isn't true that riding bitless is always kinder. Some bitless bridles exert a lot of leverage on the horse's face and jaw and some riders apply a lot of pressure even using those designed to employ less leverage.

- Any bit must be suitable for the shape of the horse's mouth, the level at which he is working and the rider's ability. It must also be the correct size and adjusted at the correct height.

- It is simplistic to say that some bits are more severe than others. Some bits have the potential to have a more severe action, but it all depends on whether the rider has a balanced, independent seat and kind hands. You can't have kind hands without an independent seat!

- A horse must be comfortable in his mouth, which is why regular dental checks and, when necessary, remedial work are vital.

- All riders should understand the actions of different mouthpieces and cheekpieces. They should also understand how a bit's action may be affected by other tack, such as a noseband or martingale.

- Competitors must be aware of rules affecting the choice of bits. The obvious example is dressage.

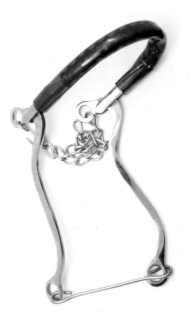

▲ Some designs of bitless bridle have the potential for considerable leverage to be exerted.

I don't believe in changing bits for the sake of it. There may be circumstances in which you need to use one with a different action, but if a horse is trained to go correctly in a simple snaffle, you should be able to stick to that. A lot of riders have problems when jumping because they use a bit which the horse backs off from, so they can't ride forwards and in a rhythm. If your horse tanks into fences, go back to the drawing board with flatwork and gridwork. Using grids is the solution to most if not all jumping problems.

CHECKING A HORSE'S MOUTH

Checking for injury

Don't just leave it to your vet or EDT to check your horse's mouth: do it yourself and do it regularly. You won't be able to inspect the mouth and teeth in as much detail as the professionals, because you won't have access to a dental gag and you won't have the same level of expertise, but you can still spot minor problems and, hopefully, call in a professional to prevent them becoming major ones.

Raise the lips gently to make sure they and the gums are in good condition. If you tickle the horse's tongue or press down on the bars of the mouth, the horse will open his mouth and may also stick out his tongue, allowing you to see obvious rubs, nicks or ulcers. Don't pull the horse's tongue through the side

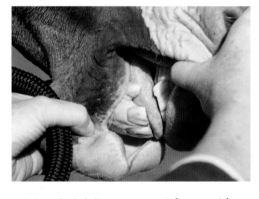

▲ Raise a horse's lips to check lips and gums for signs of damage.

of his mouth unless your vet or EDT has shown you how to do it safely. You're more likely to get bitten, albeit by a horse who doesn't mean to close his mouth on your hand but can't avoid doing so.

Check the corners of the lips for cracks or rubs. Some horses are more sensitive than others and applying petroleum jelly or even haemorrhoid cream to the corners of the mouth will help. Haemorrhoid cream is anti-inflammatory, but you can't use it if you are competing, as it will contravene the forbidden substances regulations.

A horse with any sign of mouth injury or discomfort, however minor, should not be ridden with a bit until he has been checked by a professional. Apart from the fact that you may be adding to his discomfort, you could also be setting up problems.

Common sense should dictate that you should also check the condition of any bits used, especially if you spot a problem. Some materials may be damaged by a horse's teeth, leading to rubs. Cheap bits may not be as well-made as more expensive ones; faults to look out for include rough edges round the holes of loose-ring snaffles and bits which allow more play on one cheek than the other.

Mouth conformation and bitting

Be aware of a horse's mouth conformation as well as the state of his mouth, as this will help you find a bit which suits him. There are various points to take into consideration.

- It's often said that a thicker mouthpiece is kinder than a thinner one, but this isn't necessarily the case. A thicker mouthpiece gives a greater bearing surface, but if a horse doesn't have room in his mouth for it, he will be uncomfortable. Cobs, native ponies and some crosses often have thick tongues. This reduces the amount of room available in the mouth and, as long as the rider is established enough, some horses go better with a thinner mouthpiece.

- Some horses and ponies have mouths which are relatively short from the corners of the lips to the end of the muzzle. This means that the centre of a single-jointed bit may rest too low, but a double-jointed, multi-jointed, mullen or port-mouthed one should suit.

- Some breeds, including pure-bred Arabs, Connemaras and Trakehners, often have low palates. This means that the action of a single-jointed bit will often not suit them and again, a double-jointed, multi-jointed, mullen or port-mouthed one will be better.

PERSONAL FAVOURITES

I've collected many bits over the years and normally use either a snaffle or a double bridle. Some riders and trainers like to use Pelhams and whilst I accept that some horses may go well in them, I rarely need to use one. The idea of a Pelham is that it should combine the action of the two bits which comprise a double bridle in a single mouthpiece, but in practice, it is much more vague.

The snaffles I use most often are ones with a central lozenge in the mouthpiece and multi-jointed Waterfords. I find that young horses find the former a comfortable introduction to being ridden in a bit and may be happy with it for the rest of their ridden careers. It has the advantage of being permitted under dressage rules. I don't use or like breaking bits with keys, because they encourage a horse to fiddle with the mouthpiece and may encourage him to try to put his tongue over the bit.

The Waterford mouthpiece, which unfortunately isn't dressage-legal, follows the inner conformation of any horse's mouth, which must be why so many like it. In some cases, I've used a curb with a Waterford

▼ Many horses readily accept a Waterford mouthpiece, which follows the conformation of the mouth.

mouthpiece as part of a double bridle. A bit with a Waterford mouthpiece must only be used by established riders who will not inadvertently move it from side to side across the horse's mouth. If I have any doubts, I advise riders to use a snaffle with a central lozenge instead.

SIZE AND ADJUSTMENT

All horses must be looked at as individuals when deciding on bit size and adjustment. Don't assume that the taller the horse, the larger the bit size he will require. It doesn't work like that and you may find a 16.2hh horse with a small muzzle needs a smaller bit than a chunky 14.2hh pony.

The width (i.e. 'size') of a bit mouthpiece is measured as shown in the photo opposite and the diameter is that of the widest part, near the cheeks or rings.

Some finer points of design

The type of ring or cheekpiece will affect a bit's action. For instance, a loose-ring design affords more play on the mouthpiece than a fixed cheek such as an eggbutt, full cheek or D-ring. A full

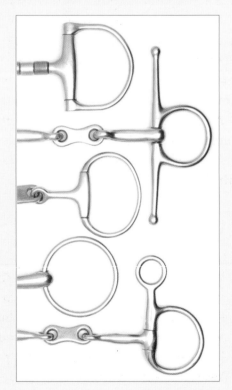

cheek or D-ring may help with steering by applying pressure against the side of the face, which is why many trainers like them for young horses at the start of their education. However, I tend to prefer loose-ring bits because they suit my riding style and I don't usually have any problems using them. A hanging-cheek snaffle applies a little poll pressure, but more importantly, takes pressure off the tongue, which some horses prefer.

When choosing a bit, take the rider's ability and preference into account. A rider with unsteady hands will cause less discomfort whilst learning if the horse is ridden in a bit which remains as still as possible in the mouth, such as an eggbutt snaffle. However, an experienced rider who niggles at the reins because a horse ridden in such a bit seems too fixed will be better using one with loose rings.

▶ The design of a cheekpiece will affect a bit's action. From the top are: D-ring, full cheek, eggbutt, loose-ring and hanging-cheek.

Pelhams and curbs can be found in a choice of cheek lengths and obviously the longer the cheek, the more potential leverage could be exerted. Cheeks are measured from top to bottom, as also shown, and the standard proportion is that the cheek is the same length, or size, as the mouthpiece. Some trainers like to use shorter (Tom Thumb) cheekpieces for a sensitive horse.

A mouthpiece must be wide enough to prevent pinching, but not so wide that it slides and bangs against the horse's lips. Many riders use a bit that is too wide; this also means that it won't lie correctly in the mouth.

To see whether a jointed bit is the correct size, straighten it in the horse's mouth. With a loose-ring snaffle, there should be no more than 1cm (0.4in) between the hole on each side and the horse's lips. A bit with fixed cheeks can fit more closely, but must not pinch. An unjointed bit should fit snugly into the corners of the mouth without pinching.

A bit must also be adjusted so that it sits at the correct height. It's often recommended that there should be a proscribed number of wrinkles at the corners of the mouth, but this doesn't work – fleshy lips, as are often found on cobs, wrinkle more easily.

▲ *left* How to measure the width of a mouthpiece in a loose-ring (top) and fixed-cheek (bottom) snaffle.

▲ *right* Pelham and curb cheeks are measured from top to bottom and obviously the longer the cheek, the more potential leverage could be exerted. Width is measured as shown.

Acceptance of the bit

Whatever bit you use, treat every horse's mouth as if it is made from china and could break. You can never force an outline; he must be educated correctly so that he accepts the bit and relaxes through the jaw. This gives what the dressage rule book calls 'submission', a term I don't actually like because it could imply force. I prefer to think of 'relaxed acceptance and co-operation'.

Instead, adjust the bit so that it fits snugly into the corners of the mouth, then ask the horse to open his mouth and see where the mouthpiece lies. It should lie across the bars and tongue without coming into contact with his canine teeth (although canine teeth are usually found in geldings, you occasionally see them in mares). If the mouthpiece has a single joint or a central lozenge or plate, this should lie on the centre of the tongue.

INTRODUCING AND FITTING A DOUBLE BRIDLE

In a correctly fitted double bridle, the bradoon sits on top of and in front of the curb and fits snugly into the corners of the mouth. The curb sits just below it.

▲ A correctly fitted double bridle, with lip strap.

Standard advice for fitting a curb chain is that it should come into play when the curb or Pelham cheek is brought back to an angle of 45 degrees, but you may need to tighten or loosen it slightly to suit a particular horse or rider.

I will only introduce a double when a horse is happy in the mouth in a snaffle and will relax and give in his jaw when a light rein aid is applied. Fit the bridle and let the horse get used to the feeling of two bits in his mouth, then start by riding purely on the bradoon so that there is nothing but the weight of the rein on the curb. When you are ready to use the curb as an extra signal to the horse to give through his jaw, touch and release; don't apply prolonged pressure. Use either the bradoon or the curb rein, not both at the same time.

I prefer to school in snaffles at home, but it's important to introduce a double bridle correctly and give the horse time to get used to its action.

If a horse doesn't have enough room in his mouth for two bits, which can occasionally be the case, a Pelham may be preferable. I don't like straight-bar Pelhams, because you often end up with a horse putting his tongue over the mouthpiece if a rider is not experienced enough to give and take. I will sometimes use a Pelham with a lozenge mouthpiece for pupils who are not quite ready to ride in a double bridle, as its vaguer action can actually be an advantage when someone is learning to manipulate double reins.

Bradoons and curbs are available with so many mouthpieces that, so far, I've been able to find a double bridle combination for any horse. For instance, I have a hunter who didn't seem to settle until I tried him in a curb with a Waterford mouthpiece, which he accepted immediately. Curbs with forward-facing ports are also useful, as they allow room for a large or fleshy tongue.

I would never use a curb with a high, upright port. The idea of using a bit that could press into the roof of a horse's mouth is horrific and it's also possible that the horse's tongue could become trapped in this type of port.

Many horses go well in a standard double link curb chain, but some sensitive animals may prefer elastic ones. Polo curb chains, which have wide, flat links, give a wide bearing surface which some horses accept more readily than other designs. I rarely use anything other than a metal curb chain, as I find I can alter the adjustment to suit most horses. Traditionally, a double bridle or Pelham should always be used with a lip strap, though some riders no longer bother. A lip strap helps to keep the curb chain in the correct place.

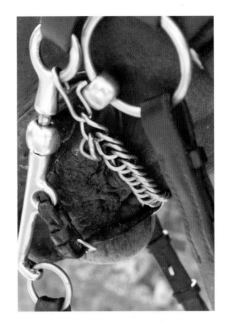

▲ A lip strap helps keep a curb chain in the correct place.

BRIDLES AND NOSEBANDS

In general, riders have become more aware of the importance of saddle fitting. Unfortunately, many don't pay the same attention to the bridles they use. Key points are:

- The browband should be long enough not to pinch the base of the ears but not so long that it flops about and irritates the horse.

- The throatlatch should not be so tight that it affects the horse's ability to flex. You should be able to fit a hand's width between the throatlatch and the horse's face.

- Nosebands should not be so high that they rub the facial bones. If you use a Grakle, Flash or drop it should be adjusted to discourage the horse from opening his mouth too wide, but not to strap it shut. If a horse can't flex his jaws, he can't work on the bit. I never use nosebands designed to double back so that they can be fastened as tight as possible, sometimes called cinch, winch or doubleback nosebands. They prevent a horse flexing his jaws and must cause discomfort.

- A noseband that is too tight also puts pressure on the poll, so check the fit of the bridle behind the ears as well as round the nose and muzzle.

▲ The browband should be long enough not to pinch the base of the ears but not so long that it flops about and irritates the horse.

THE GRAKLE

I prefer a high-ring Grakle to a Flash or drop noseband and use one as standard when schooling a horse at home in a snaffle. It is effective without being too restrictive and does not put pressure on the cheek teeth, making it an excellent choice for young horses who are still cutting adult teeth. As well as teaching a horse to keep his jaw soft without restricting him, it discourages those who curl their tongues back under the bit from doing so. These lessons will carry on when you introduce the horse to a double bridle.

When I'm using a Grakle, I adjust it so I can easily slip a finger behind both the top and the bottom straps. This will discourage the horse from opening his mouth too wide or crossing his jaw, but won't prevent him relaxing his jaw and mouthing the bit.

Unfortunately, the Grakle isn't permitted under British Dressage rules, though it is allowed for horse trials tests, so if you take your horse out to dressage competitions run under BD rules you will have to use a cavesson, drop or Flash noseband. If you use a Flash, the upper (cavesson) part must be substantial enough to stay in place when the bottom strap is fastened, or it will slip down the horse's face. A drop noseband should be adjusted so it does not interfere with the horse's breathing.

SADDLE CHOICE AND FIT

A saddle must fit the horse, fit the rider and be fit for purpose. Many riders will need professional advice on choice and fitting, but be careful from whom that advice originates! The fact that a top rider enthuses about a particular design doesn't necessarily mean it will suit you, even if you intend to use it for the same discipline – and buying a saddle endorsed by a successful rider doesn't, sadly, mean you will be able to ride like him or her.

In most cases, the best person to advise you will be a saddler who has wide experience of all disciplines, has a practical knowledge of riding to a good level and can assess horse and rider combinations at all levels. That may be easier said than done, so take time to find the right person and don't begrudge paying for their time. The Society of Master Saddlers offers a saddle-fitting qualification and whilst there are good fitters who don't hold it, you know that someone who does has been shown to have a good level of knowledge.

Try different types and makes of saddle before deciding what works for you. A saddle should help your riding position and balance, not hinder it, but not all are designed with the same level of expertise. For instance, if the stirrup bars are set too far forward or too far back, you'll struggle to ride in balance.

A professional saddle-fitter will help you find the right saddle and adjust or balance it so it fits your horse at that time. The problem is that horses change shape rapidly as they gain or lose weight or muscle and a saddle that fits perfectly to start with won't necessarily do the same a few months or even weeks later. Therefore, all riders need to understand the basics of correct saddle fit so they know when to call on professional advice. Booking routine saddle checks twice a year is better than nothing, but may not be enough to keep your horse comfortable, sound and working well.

Most saddles are built on trees and these remain the most popular choice. The tree must be the correct width and profile for a particular horse and the best way to assess this is to take a profile of the withers using a Flexicurve, a flexible template used by architects and draughtsmen. Some saddle trees are adjustable, but usually this will only be at the front. They are useful in some cases, but do not provide a universal answer.

Ideally, every horse should have his own saddle, but this isn't possible on large yards with changing horse populations. Here, it's important to have a selection of saddles so that the best fit can be achieved.

Riders often say that they have a saddle that 'fits everything'. It may have the potential to fit every animal they own, but chances are that this is because all their horses are of the same type. As a show producer, I know that the saddle that fits a wide cob definitely will not fit an ex-racehorse who is much narrower and has a different back and withers profile.

▲ The easiest way to take a saddle-fitting template is to use a Flexicurve.

There are situations in which treeless saddles may be appropriate and there may be horses and riders for whom the right, correctly balanced treeless saddle is ideal. Unfortunately, too many riders assume that a treeless saddle can be placed on any horse and will automatically fit. It won't: it will usually need balancing with the use of pads and/or shims.

ASSESSING FIT – THE HORSE

To assess saddle fit, you need an observant helper or, if you prefer to take the observer role, a rider who is roughly the same height, shape and weight as yourself. Place the saddle on the horse, girth up and check that the centre of the seat is the lowest point. If not, the rider will be tipped backwards or forwards.

Is the saddle in the right place? This might sound obvious, but a common mistake is to position it too far forward. As a horse moves, the top of his shoulder-blade (scapula) rotates backwards and a saddle that is wrongly placed will impede his movement. There should be a hand's width between the shoulder-blade and the saddle.

Mounting

When mounting, always use a mounting block when possible. Getting on from the ground puts strain on the saddle tree and can eventually twist it. It also puts strain on the horse's back. Many riders pull the saddle to the left when mounting, then heave it over by putting more weight in the right stirrup. Alternatively, get a leg-up.

With any design of saddle, key fitting points are:

■ With a rider on board, the saddle should be level from front to back and the rider should be balanced, without being tipped forwards or backwards. This applies whether the saddle has a straight or forward cut – but if the stirrup bars are positioned wrongly, the rider may find it hard to adopt a balanced seat naturally.

■ Stand behind the horse to see if the saddle sits evenly, or is more to one side than the other. If it is lopsided, check that the stirrup leathers are the same length and that the rider isn't putting more weight in one stirrup than the other without realising. Also from the back, check that the saddle gullet is clear of the horse's back all the way along, including under the rider.

■ The pommel and cantle must clear the withers and back respectively, both when the rider is seated and when standing in the stirrups. The amount of clearance needed depends on the design of the saddle and its purpose – you usually need greater clearance for jumping than for flatwork. Well-designed close-contact jumping saddles, which are constructed to ensure that there is as little as possible between the rider and the horse, can still satisfy clearance requirements.

■ The panel should give as even a bearing surface as possible and the saddle shouldn't bounce noticeably or swing from side to side when the horse is moving. There is bound to be some movement, because the saddle is the interface between the horse's movement and the rider trying to absorb it, but it shouldn't be excessive.

■ Horse and rider should be assessed in all gaits, on both reins. Does the saddle look as if it sits correctly on circles and turns as well as on straight lines? If it is used for jumping, does it stay reasonably stable through all phases of the jump?

■ The horse's reactions can give clues to his comfort. If he shows signs of resistance, perhaps when turning in one direction or when making transitions, could the saddle be pinching or moving too much? The saddle may, of course, be nothing to do with it, but solving problems means looking at all parts of the jigsaw and saddle fit is one of them.

ASSESSING FIT – THE RIDER

A saddle must fit the rider as well as the horse. If its proportions do not complement yours, you will be insecure and an unbalanced rider means an unbalanced horse, so take both of your needs into account. However, the horse's needs come first.

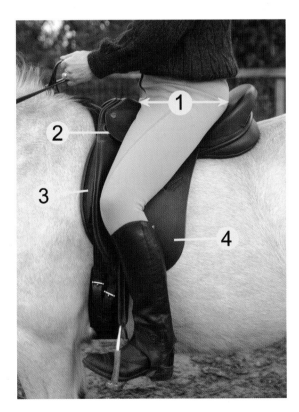

▶ A saddle must suit the rider's proportions as well as fitting the horse.

1. Seat is the correct size and puts rider in the centre of the saddle.

2. Stirrup bars are sited to allow a correct leg position.

3. Knee blocks are positioned to allow the rider's leg to sit just behind them.

4. Flaps are the correct length for the rider's leg proportions.

Make sure that the design is suitable not just for your purpose, but for your level of riding and preferences. For instance, some riders like large knee rolls and others prefer to be able to adapt their position. Stirrup bars must be sited so they encourage a correct position: while they should be placed more forward on a jumping saddle, they need to be further back on a dressage or general-purpose model. Many general-purpose saddles feature stirrup bars that naturally place the rider's leg forward of the ideal shoulder-hip-heel vertical alignment. This leaves the rider either with a 'chair' seat that shifts their balance backwards, or fighting the natural forces of physics by trying to bring their legs back against the pull of the stirrups. Other points to consider are:

■ Does the seat size suit your own? Seats are measured in half-inch increments, but other proportions alter accordingly and a rider who feels secure in a 17in saddle may not do so in the next size up.

■ Does the twist (the area from the pommel to the centre of the seat) suit your conformation and preferred discipline?

■ Are the flaps the right size for your proportions? If you are buying a new saddle, it may be possible to have shorter or longer flaps than standard to take your proportions into account.

Many riders put more weight on one stirrup than the other, which unbalances the horse. As a temporary or, if necessary, permanent measure your expert may adjust your saddle slightly on one side to compensate; riding with one stirrup leather a hole shorter than the other is an even quicker temporary fix, but don't look on it as a permanent solution. Of course, if a rider has a condition which means one leg is actually or effectively shorter than the other, he or she will need stirrup leathers adjusting at different lengths to establish a correct balance. If you know you habitually ride lopsided but don't know why, it's well worth consulting a qualified practitioner such as a chartered physiotherapist. You may find your fault can be corrected.

If your saddle slips to one side, it isn't necessarily down to you. Horses can be one-sided, perhaps because one hind leg is weaker than the other, through undetected lameness or simply because they can naturally be more supple on one rein than the other. Correct schooling can make a huge difference but, if a horse is crooked, he may push his saddle – and you – over to one side even when the saddle is properly adjusted. I've had one top-class horse who did this to a marked degree and although he showed no obvious signs of pain or discomfort, was given a course of shockwave therapy in the back area on veterinary advice. This made a real difference and it was then much easier to even everything up.

SADDLES FOR PONIES

Adult riders of average stature riding ponies must take the length of a pony's back into account when choosing saddles. This isn't usually a problem with the larger native breeds, but can affect those riding small or particularly short-backed animals. The best strategy is to consult a good saddler fitter, who should be able to help by finding a saddle with short enough panels.

Some riders prefer saddles with suede seats and flaps because they find this gives greater security. These are particularly popular for show ponies. However, don't look on a suede finish as compensation for a saddle that isn't designed to help the rider.

If you're buying a saddle for a child, it's vital that it helps rather than hinders a small rider. Too often – especially in the showing world – you see small children plonked on dinner plate saddles that do them no favours and, if they feel insecure, they won't enjoy their riding.

SADDLE ACCESSORIES

Pads and numnahs

When working at home, I usually use a single thickness, padded cotton square to help keep a horse comfortable, without interfering with the fit of the saddle. It's easy to wash and allows us to keep our expensive sheepskin numnahs for shows. I don't like thicker pads because they make it more likely that a saddle will roll.

Whatever type of pad or numnah you use, it should be fitted so it pulls up into the saddle gullet to avoid putting pressure on the withers. It should also extend beyond the end of the panels, front and back, to avoid pressure points. If you need a design that looks discreet, it's possible to have sheepskin numnahs made to measure.

Girths

I always use an elasticated girth, again, for reasons of comfort. My schooling girths have elastic at both ends so that the 'give' is evenly distributed, as if you use one with elastic at one end only, the tension is lopsided. They also have a detachable neoprene sleeve, which has good grip properties. This helps make sure the girth and the saddle stay in the right place, and it can be taken off for washing. Tack, girth and rugs must be kept clean, or you run the risk of skin rubs or infections, but anything that makes washing easier has to be a good idea.

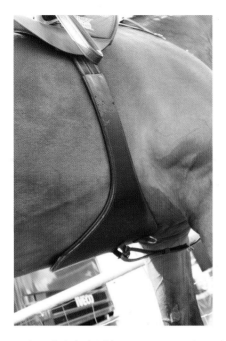

▲ A stud girth should prevent a horse from injuring himself if he snaps up his forelegs over a fence.

Don't over-tighten a girth. This will make the horse uncomfortable and can restrict his stride and cause him to buck when you first get on. If your saddle slips, check that it fits correctly and use a girth or girth sleeve with good grip properties.

When I'm jumping, at home or in the ring, I use a stud girth. If a horse snaps up his forelegs and catches his belly with shoes or studs, he may bruise or cut himself. At the very least, he'll cause himself discomfort, which may make him reluctant to jump because he associates it with something unpleasant.

Stirrup irons

Your choice of stirrup iron design is a matter of personal preference. Many people use safety irons as standard and bent leg safety irons or flexi-irons are recommended. Peacock safety irons, with a rubber ring on the outside, should only be used for very small children. If used by larger riders, the extra weight can stress the metal to breaking point.

Stirrup irons must be of an appropriate size for the rider's foot. They must be large enough to allow about 6–7mm (¼in) at *each* side of the rider's foot. The measurement should be taken at the widest part of the rider's boot. Don't allow children to ride with stirrup irons meant for adults if there is a danger that their feet could slip through. (Similarly, don't let children ride with adult-size

◄ Bent leg safety irons, shown here, or flexi-irons, are recommended for safety.

► Peacock safety irons should only be used by very small children, as the extra weight of larger riders may stress the metal to breaking point – as happened here.

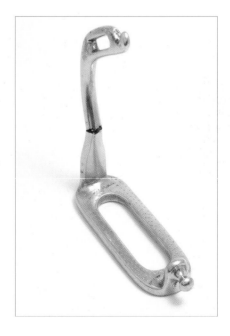

reins, as there is a risk that they could put a foot through the loop. Buy pony-size reins for pony-size riders.)

TRAINING AIDS

The use of training aids or gadgets is always a controversial topic and certainly they should be used with caution: there is potential for any equipment, including classical training aids such as side-reins, to cause discomfort if they are wrongly adjusted. Apart from the lungeing system described in Chapter 12, the only training aid I use as standard is a Market Harborough, which I often fit when horses go hacking.

The Market Harborough is a cross between a rein and a martingale that encourages a horse to go in a correct but still relaxed outline without restricting him. It fastens to the girth, then splits into two straps which pass through the snaffle rings and clip to small D-rings on the reins. It must be fitted so that the ordinary reins come into effect before the Market Harborough straps, so it only comes into play if the horse raises his head too high. As soon as he responds to its action, the rein releases without the rider having to do anything, so the horse rewards himself.

I don't use a Market Harborough on children's ponies, but if a pony snatches at the reins I use my version of grass reins. I fit side-reins so they cross at the withers and attach to the D-rings on the saddle, adjusting them so they are short enough to prevent the pony yanking at the rider, but not so short that they pull

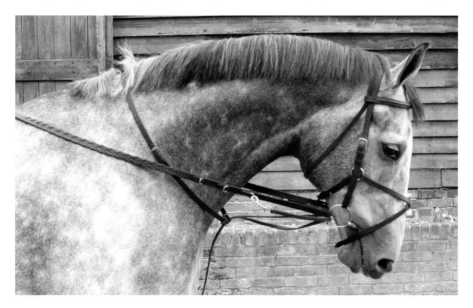

◄ A correctly fitted Market Harborough.

in the animal's head. A child who has to ride a pony who pulls and yanks loses the ability to ride with soft hands and often starts pulling back.

I don't like equipment that relies on the rider to release it, such as draw reins. These rely on split-second timing – and how many riders, even the best, can guarantee to meet that requirement every time? I won't say I've never used draw reins, but if I have, it's been for a very short period, with great care and for a particular reason.

TACK CLEANING AND MAINTENANCE

Check tack regularly for signs of wear and tear, paying special attention to stitching and any areas where metal rests on leather. Girth straps and stirrup leathers take a lot of strain. Bits should also be checked for signs of wear.

If your saddle has conventional flocking, run your hands over the panels to make sure it has not become lumpy. If necessary, get it checked and adjusted by your saddler before using it again, or you'll cause a pressure point on your horse's back. Always get a saddle which has been dropped or rolled on checked, because if the tree has been damaged it can cause serious damage to your horse.

Ideally, leather tack should be cleaned after every use. If this is impossible – and it isn't something I always manage – wash the bit to prevent saliva and food debris drying on it and check and clean the areas where metal rests on leather. Dismantle tack once a week to clean and check it and, if necessary, apply leather food. You shouldn't need to apply leather food every week and overdoing it can weaken leather by causing the fibres to stretch.

Here are some tack-cleaning tips from professional grooms:

■ Bits and stirrup irons can be washed in a dishwasher if you want them to be super-clean and shiny.

■ Use a cocktail stick to remove dirt and excess cleaner or soap from holes in straps and stirrup leathers.

■ Apply leather food to the rough (flesh) side of the leather. If you apply it to the smooth side, it won't be absorbed.

■ If you buy new tack, check the manufacturer's instructions regarding care. This applies to synthetic as well as leather tack, because if you use saddle soap or leather dressing on synthetic tack you could damage it.

■ Muddy tack can be dunked – but not soaked – in a bucket of hand-hot water, and mud sponged off. Wet tack, including that which has got soaked by rain, should be dried off at room temperature. Don't dry tack directly in front of a heater or radiator, or it will become brittle. Once it's dry, clean and feed leather.

■ Unless the manufacturer's instructions state otherwise, sheepskin products should be dried naturally, brushed off to remove loose hairs and caked sweat and washed. You may have to wash them by hand, using a recommended product.

Tack theft is all too common, so take security seriously. Yards should think about installing alarm systems and CCTV cameras, and tack should be marked with your postcode. An easy way to mark it is to engrave your postcode on metal items and fittings such as stirrup bars, stirrup irons and buckles.

KEY POINTS

- Bits must be suitable for the shape of the horse's mouth, the level at which he is working and the rider's ability. They must also be the correct size and adjusted at the correct height.

- There is no such thing as a magic bit, but understanding the action of mouthpieces and cheekpieces will help you to choose one which is likely to be most suitable.

- A saddle must fit the horse, fit the rider and be fit for purpose.

- Ideally, every horse should have his own saddle, but this isn't possible on large yards with changing horse populations. Here, it's important to have a selection of saddles so that the best fit can be achieved.

- Numnahs should be correctly sized and adjusted to avoid the risk of pressure points.

- Stirrup irons must be of an appropriate size for the rider's foot – large enough to allow about 6–7mm (¼in) at each side of the rider's foot.

- Don't allow children to use adult-size stirrup irons if there is a danger that their feet could slip through.

- Don't allow children to use adult-size reins, as there is a risk they could put a foot through the loop and get caught up.

- Appropriate safety irons are a must for children and recommended for all riders.

The Last Word

As you've worked your way through this book, I hope it's become clear that good horse management is a jigsaw with lots of pieces and that modern management is a mixture of traditional and new skills. Be observant, whether you are dealing with a horse you know well or one who has just come to your yard. When I run clinics, I find that small changes can make a big difference: simply altering the height of a bit by one hole can make a difference to a horse's way of going.

Never ignore changes in a horse's demeanour. I don't mean you need to be worried if a horse seems particularly bright on the first cold day of the year – in fact, I'd be more worried if he wasn't! But if he suddenly seems subdued, or grumpy, there will be a reason for it.

Be open to new ideas, but don't assume that they are always better. If you know your horse and know he's happy and content, don't change things just for the sake of it.

If in doubt, ask advice, but ask the right people. You should have a network of experts you can rely on; it might be interesting to listen to or read discussions, but just because someone sounds convincing, it doesn't mean he or she knows more than the professionals you rely on.

It's a privilege as well as a pleasure to look after horses. None of us can get it right all the time, but we should always do our best.

Further Reading

This book contains information about many aspects of horse management. The authors suggest that readers wanting to find out more about particular topics would enjoy the following books.

Getting Horses Fit by Carolyn Henderson (J. A. Allen) ISBN 978 0 85131 897 4

Horse Tack Bible by Carolyn Henderson (David and Charles) ISBN 978 0 7153 2879 8

Katie Jerram on Showing by Katie Jerram and Carolyn Henderson (J. A. Allen) ISBN 978 0 85131 989 6

Design Handbook for Stables and Equestrian Buildings by Keith Warth (J. A. Allen) ISBN 978 1 908809 18 6

The Truth About Feeding Your Horse by Clare MacLeod (J. A. Allen) ISBN 978 0 85131 918 6

Index